CLIMBING THE

CORPORATE LADDER

CLIMBING THE CORPORATE LADDER

What You Need to Know and Do
to Be a Promotable Person

Barbara Pachter
Marjorie Brody

SkillPath Publications
Mission, Kansas

Editor: Kelly Scanlon

Cover and Book Design: Rod Hankins, David Sherer

Library of Congress Catalog Card Number: 95-69804

ISBN: 1-878542-85-0

10   9   8   7   6   5   4   3   2   1   95   96   97   98   99

Printed in the United States of America

CONTENTS

INTRODUCTION

James Treybig, president of Tandem Computers, once said that there are three kinds of people:

- People who make things happen.
- People who watch things happen.
- People who get knocked over the head and then say, "What happened?"

Which kind of person are you?

Obviously, if you're reading this book, you're a person who's making things happen. And one of the things you're going to find out about is how to make things happen in your career.

First of all, it's important to recognize that there's a difference between having a job and having a career. Having a job means going to work and collecting your paycheck. There's little concern about opportunities for promotion to higher levels within or outside of the organization.

A career, on the other hand, demands much more attention. Career-oriented people are concerned not only about accomplishing the tasks within their current realm of responsibility but also about finding ways to attain higher positions.

In today's working environment, the path to promotion—or even to keeping your job—is not always clear or certain. One day, you think you have a handle on it. The next day the entire scenario may change. The days of promotion by virtue of seniority have ended. Just putting in your time and doing your job are no longer enough to keep you climbing the corporate ladder.

Today's worker is also facing more competition than ever before. Colleges and graduate schools are constantly turning out bright-eyed, eager graduates—and all of them want to put their skills and knowledge to work. Add to that the growing number of highly skilled professionals with years of experience who suddenly find themselves looking for new jobs as the result of organizational downsizing, relocation, or closing. Consider, for example, the consultant for a pharmaceutical company who wanted job security. When he was offered an internal position with the company, he took it. Nine months later, the parent company sold his division. Three months after that, he was out of a job!

So, how can one individual—even the most Promotable Person—ever hope to climb the corporate ladder when the ground underneath it keeps shifting and there are so many competitors fighting for a place on every rung? It's true that it is more difficult than ever to move ahead in today's corporate environment. But it's not impossible. Not if you're ready and able to take responsibility for your own promotability. The Promotable Person knows how to recognize, take advantage of, and even create opportunities to stand out from the crowd.

Climbing the Corporate Ladder consists of twelve chapters divided into four parts.

In Part 1, you'll assess your potential for being promoted and learn how to take charge of your career by setting goals and finding mentors.

In Part 2, you'll zero in on ways to improve your leadership skills, the importance of becoming an expert, and how to avoid the power robbers of stress, lack of time management, and the inability to take risks.

Part 3 focuses on one of the most important skills you must master if you're a Promotable Person—communication skills. The three chapters in this section cover speaking and writing skills, assertive communication, giving and receiving feedback, and networking.

In Part 4, you'll get pointers on how to make a good impression, including business standards for wardrobe and grooming, good manners, use of office equipment, and etiquette tips for conducting business internationally.

In the final chapter, you'll learn how to ask for a raise and promotion. You'll also find out how to cope as you continue your climb up the ladder, even if you're rejected for promotion.

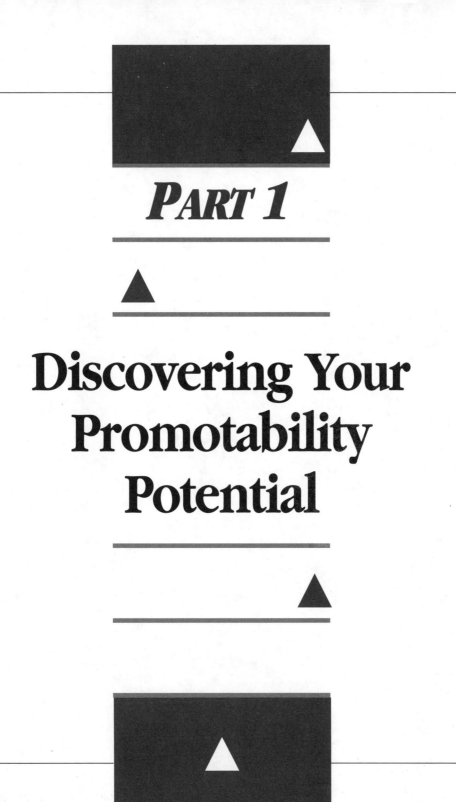

PART 1

Discovering Your Promotability Potential

▲ CHAPTER 1

Are You a Promotable Person?

So you want to get promoted. Other people are—and, no, they can't all be related to their bosses. They don't seem to be any more intelligent than you are. Or more talented. Or more hard-working. Then what do they have that you don't have? What do they know that you don't know?

Before you learn their secrets, wouldn't you like to find out how promotable you already are? Take the Promotable Person Quiz and find out. Just answer "yes" or "no" to the following questions.

Exercise 1

PROMOTABLE PERSON QUIZ

	Yes	No
1. Do you have career goals?	☐	☐
2. Do you know people inside and outside of your organization who can help you and from whom you can learn?	☐	☐
3. Are you an expert recognized as a knowledge resource:		
• Within your organization?	☐	☐
• Within your industry?	☐	☐
4. Do you convey a professional image?	☐	☐
5. Do you communicate effectively with others when you:		
• Write?	☐	☐
• Speak?	☐	☐
6. Do you effectively manage your stress?	☐	☐
7. Do you effectively manage your time?	☐	☐
8. Are you a risk-taker?	☐	☐
9. Do you see yourself as a problem-solver?	☐	☐
10. Do you stand up for yourself?	☐	☐
11. Do you understand the politics of your organization?	☐	☐
12. Are you taking responsibility for your promotability?	☐	☐

Obviously, your answer to all these questions should be "yes." Each question represents one or more aspects of the skills, traits, and actions that characterize the Promotable Person. But even if you didn't answer yes to all twelve questions, that doesn't mean you don't have the potential to be a Promotable Person. The very fact that you're reading this book shows that you have the *desire* to be promoted. That's the first step. Now read on to find out how to develop the skills you need to enhance your promotability.

WHY PEOPLE GET PROMOTED

There are many reasons why people get promoted. Consider these:

- Tom Smith got promoted to supervisor in a different department because he responded to a job posting and knew his future boss from the company softball team.

- Susan Jamansin asked for feedback on her professional presence and was advised to cut her hair. She did. Three months later, she was promoted. The only thing that had changed was the length of her hair—nothing else.

- A researcher in an engineering firm was promoted after volunteering to represent her company by speaking at a national conference. She did a great job.

- Dan Martinson was simply in the right place at the right time: two companies merged, Dan's department expanded, and after six months of increased responsibility, he was promoted.

Sometimes things just happen. Sometimes people make them happen. But, in all these cases, individuals were prepared to take advantage of or create opportunities to stand out, take charge, and get noticed.

UNDERSTANDING THE DYNAMICS OF YOUR WORKPLACE

As you start down the path to promotion, take a little time to study the lay of the land. Every organization has its own culture, its own politics, its own hierarchy. Understanding the dynamics of your workplace often allows you to take advantage of or create opportunities for promotion. Do you thoroughly understand yours? Here are some tips to help you:

1. **Analyze your boss.** Does he or she help employees move up? There is one department within a particular government agency that people actually fight to get into. The manager, a lawyer, always works with his people to move them along in their careers within the agency.

2. **Analyze your organization's job-changing and promotion process.** Is there a formal system? Are all job openings posted? Must you establish a relationship with an employee representative? Find out.

3. Discover who really has power within your organization. It's not necessarily the people who hold the highest positions or the biggest titles. The people with power are those who make things happen either by doing them or by influencing others. Sometimes these powerful people may be only a couple of rungs above you on the corporate ladder. Or they may be your co-workers. Or they may even hold positions a rung or two below yours.

Whoever these people are, you want to know them. Just as important, you want them to know you.

Still, just *knowing* the right people won't guarantee you a promotion. You must have the skills and ability to do the job. On the other hand, you can have all the right qualifications and still not get the promotion if the right people don't know about you. If that's the case, then no matter how wonderful you are, you might as well be invisible.

4. Identify the individuals within your organization who have already established themselves as Promotable People. Ask yourself these questions about those people:

- What skills do these people have?

- What people do they know?

- What did they do to make the promotion happen?

Over time, your answers to these questions should reveal patterns that will tell you a lot about your organization. Once you understand these patterns, you can apply this information to yourself to determine where you want your career to go and what you have to do to achieve your goals.

For example, if you are a secretary and want to move up to management, what has to occur in your organization? What do *you* need to do? Do you need to take college courses, transfer to another department, or perhaps leave the company?

If you are an engineer and want to become a manager, what has to occur in your organization? What do *you* need to do? Do you have to take a position overseas, get management development training, or get the attention of certain people within your organization?

The realities of your workplace will, of course, dictate what you need to do to achieve your career goals. But once you know what those realities are, you have the power to make choices. Then it's up to you. Are you up to the challenge? Are you willing to do what it takes to succeed?

If your answer is "yes," then you're ready to move on and learn the secrets of the people in today's workplace who are getting ahead.

PROMOTABLE ASSIGNMENTS

1. Create a "promotable diary." Write down the names of the individuals within your organization or within your division who have been promoted in the last six to twelve months. Analyze this list of names by asking yourself the questions on page 10.

2. Identify the formal job-changing and promotion system in your organization. Know where the jobs are posted. Create a routine to check the postings regularly.

▲ CHAPTER 2

Taking Charge of Your Career

Before you can plan how to get where you want to go, you have to know where you want to go. That's the first step in career planning, perhaps the most important step you will take in your professional life.

KNOW YOURSELF

Whether you're new to the job market or looking to make a move within your current company or outside of it, your best and most valuable tool is a well-organized plan. But before you begin to develop that plan, take some time to do a little soul-searching. In *Hamlet*, Shakespeare wrote, "To thine own self be true." Of course, he wasn't referring to career planning, but it's the best advice anyone could ever give the Promotable Person.

Perhaps you think you already know what you want and where you want to go. You may be right. In that case, the self-assessment that follows will confirm your conclusions. On the other hand, what you learn about yourself just may surprise you.

Exercise 2

SELF-ASSESSMENT: WHERE DO I WANT TO GO?

1. Do you perform better in an office or out in the field?

   _____

   _____

2. Do you prefer to work as part of a team or alone?

   _____

   _____

3. Would you feel more comfortable in a small company or in a large corporation?

   _____

   _____

4. Do you have entrepreneurial traits?

   _____

   _____

5. Are you more comfortable making decisions or letting others lead?

   _____

   _____

6. Do you have the need or desire to move up the corporate ladder?

   _____

   _____

7. Are you prepared to devote time and energy to your career?

   _____

   _____

Depending on how you answer these questions, you may choose to stay where you are or search for new opportunities.

If you conclude that what you want and are willing to work toward is furthering your career, the next step is to list your marketable skills and accomplishments. Use the following Marketability Analysis to help you.

Exercise 3

MARKETABILITY ANALYSIS

First, list your marketable skills and your professional accomplishments. Then identify ten reasons why you should be hired or promoted to the particular position you want (e.g., you work well with people, you use your time wisely, you're current in your knowledge of the XYZ computer, etc.).

A. List your marketable skills:

_____

_____

_____

_____

_____

_____

_____

_____

B. List your accomplishments in your field:

_____

_____

_____

_____

_____

_____

_____

_____

C. List ten reasons why you should be hired or promoted:

1. _____
2. _____
3. _____
4. _____
5. _____
6. _____
7. _____
8. _____
9. _____
10. _____

Think carefully about the words you used to describe your skills and accomplishments. This will help you to discuss them clearly on a job interview, when meeting with your boss, or as you write your résumé.

Choose words that are strong and active. Avoid weak and vague words such as *observed* or *was responsible for*. Notice that these words don't emphasize your skills and accomplishments.

Instead, select words such as *designed, implemented, saved, created, increased, established, developed,* and *directed*. If you don't yet have direct job experience, make the most of your extracurricular activities, summer or part-time work experience, or other opportunities where you've been able to demonstrate your leadership or marketable job skills.

SETTING CAREER GOALS

Before you can get to the top of the corporate ladder, you have to climb a lot of rungs. Each rung you climb represents a goal accomplished, and the one above it is the next level you could aspire to.

Setting goals is crucial for the Promotable Person. To get started, use the Goal-Setting Worksheet on the following page.

Exercise 4

GOAL-SETTING WORKSHEET

A. In the first column, write down a list of the things you'd like to achieve in your career. In the second column, list things you know you don't want.

Things I Would Like In My Career   Things I Wouldn't Like In My Career

_____   _____

_____   _____

_____   _____

_____   _____

_____   _____

_____   _____

_____   _____

B. Using the lists above as a starting point, set some short- and long-term goals. Where would you like to be in six months, twelve months, two years, five years? (Questions like these are often asked during job interviews.)

Short-Term Goals   Long-Term Goals

_____   _____

_____   _____

_____   _____

_____   _____

_____   _____

_____   _____

_____   _____

C. Analyze what you have to do in the next six months to meet your twelve-month goals, in twelve months to meet your two-year goals, and so on. This is a chance for you to analyze your strengths and realistically evaluate areas that may need strengthening. Do you need more education? Are your goals realistic?

For instance, if you're currently working as a mailroom clerk, it isn't likely that you're going to become a vice president within the next twelve months. At the same time, it doesn't mean that you can *never* become vice president of your company. If becoming a vice president is what you really want—and what you think you're capable of becoming—then, by all means, make it a goal. Just be realistic and make it a long-term goal. Use the lines below to jot down some of the actions you'll take to meet your goals.

_____

_____

_____

_____

_____

_____

_____

One final reminder about setting your goals: Be sure your personal goals are in line with the goals of both your company and upper management. For instance, will the person who currently holds the job that you want have to be promoted or leave the company in order for you to succeed? Is there room for growth within the company or will you have to leave in order to meet your goals? If the latter is the case, don't start writing your letter of resignation just yet. However, it's always to your benefit to be realistic about your long-term goals as you set them and work toward achieving them.

THE IMPORTANCE OF MENTORS

A mentor is someone who can be your guide as you make your way up the corporate ladder. It's someone who can help you map out the best and most direct routes to your goals while avoiding some of the more treacherous pitfalls. A mentor is *not* someone who will hold your hand and walk you through your career. However, a caring mentor will usually hold out a hand to help you get safely over some of the rougher spots. You may be surprised to find that even top-level professionals are willing and, in fact, flattered to be asked to share their knowledge and experience with someone less advanced in their field. Many even take great pleasure in watching and helping protégés work their way toward their career goals.

Choosing a mentor is not something you should take lightly. Nor is agreeing to become someone else's mentor (your time will come, Promotable Person, so keep this in mind). Because this relationship can be so crucial to you and your career, it's wise to do some careful research before approaching a potential mentor. Ideally, your mentor should be someone who is well-established and commands respect in your industry.

The first question to ask yourself is, "Does this person have anything to lose by helping me?" For instance, if the person you have in mind is a manager, be certain that he or she wants you to get ahead and won't feel threatened by your promotion. Keep in mind, too, that your peers may misconstrue a mentoring relationship with your boss, so proceed with caution.

If the person you choose as your mentor holds a position higher than your boss, think about how your boss might feel about it. Will such a relationship jeopardize your relationship with your boss? If so, choose another mentor.

Look around. Is there someone in your chosen field whom you particularly admire? If so, write a short letter to that person describing yourself and why it would be mutually beneficial for him or her to take an interest in you. If you're already acquainted with your prospective mentor, a call might be appropriate. Or you might prefer to ask the person for advice and let the relationship naturally develop over time.

If you are new at your company, ask when you are hired whether the company has a formal mentoring system. Some companies have peer mentoring, which means you will be assigned to someone at your own level who has been with the company for several months or more to "show you the ropes." Other firms may match you up with someone at a higher level to help show you how to succeed within the organization. If you are fortunate enough to be hired by a company that provides mentoring, be sure to take full advantage of it. In most cases, however, it's up to the Promotable Person to take the initiative to find a mentor.

As you move ahead in your career, always remember to show appreciation for the help and guidance your mentor has provided. Always acknowledge your mentor's contributions to your success. Remember to say thank you. And be ready to say yes when, sometime in the future, you're the person some up-and-coming Promotable Person chooses for a mentor.

PART 2

Honing Your "Promotable" Skills

▲ CHAPTER 3

A Lesson in Leadership

What does being a leader have to do with being a Promotable Person? Just about everything.

A leader is an individual who inspires people to do their best. So is the Promotable Person. A leader is someone who is out in front, helping his or her organization reach its immediate goals and set its course for the future. The same goes for the Promotable Person.

The word *leader* may conjure up a wide range of images for you, from Nelson Mandela to Mary Kay Ash to General Norman Schwarzkopf to the president of your local PTA. Obviously, leadership has many different faces. However, many leaders do share a number of common traits.

WHAT MAKES A LEADER?

Inspiring. Courageous. Decisive. These are some of the words traditionally used to describe leaders. But don't be discouraged if you don't feel that all—or even any—of these terms describe you at this point in your life and your career. Forget the old adage, "leaders are born, not made." Although not everyone may have what it takes to become President of the United States, every person— including you—can develop many of the qualities of leadership.

Before you can become a leader, you have to know what it takes to be one. In other words, what it is that sets leaders apart from everyone else. How do you recognize leadership traits so that you can emulate them or at least aspire to them? Here are twelve traits that leaders commonly share.

1. **Vision.** One of the most important traits leaders have is vision—the ability to think about how today's decisions and actions will affect their organizations tomorrow. But it's not enough to merely *have* vision. Leaders must be able to articulate their vision so that others will share it and help bring it into reality.

2. **Responsibility.** Leaders ensure that plans are carried out and directions are followed. Although they may delegate certain areas of responsibility, they keep themselves informed and know the outcome of actions that are taken. Perhaps most important of all, leaders are accountable, not only for their own actions, but also for the actions of the people to whom they delegate. If things go wrong, leaders will accept the blame, even if they are not directly responsible, especially when the company's reputation is at risk.

3. **Credibility.** Leaders are true to their word, and their actions are consistent with their words. They are trusted by both their allies *and* their opponents.

4. **Tenacity.** Leaders don't abandon an idea or project they truly believe in just because it becomes unpopular or difficult. In many cases, it's just this sort of situation that gives the true leader an opportunity to shine.

5. **Decisiveness.** Leaders must be able to think on their feet. They must know how to make decisions quickly, and they have the sound judgment to recognize when to act and when to hold back.

6. Loyalty. Whether or not they are in a position of power, leaders always work for the best interest of the company and its employees.

7. Ability to inspire. Leaders know how to make others feel that their efforts are important. They are able to motivate others to follow their lead in pursuing a common goal.

8. Resiliency. Leaders bounce back from failure and disappointment. Instead of giving up, leaders look for new paths to follow—or to pioneer.

9. Competitiveness. Whatever the game, leaders play it to win and are exhilarated by the challenges that come with competition.

10. Courage. When confronted, leaders are able to put aside personal doubts and fears in order to carry out a job for the good of the organization.

11. Ability to articulate. People can't act on an idea unless they know what to do. Leaders can translate ideas into words and clearly communicate those words both orally and on paper.

12. Sensitivity. Effective leaders are conscious and caring of the feelings of others. They understand that people need to feel worthwhile and respond best to positive reinforcement.

Successful leaders don't necessarily possess all twelve of these traits. However, they do have most of them. And there are three traits that anyone who ever aspires to leadership must have: credibility, responsibility, and decisiveness. These are also the traits that no Promotable Person can afford to be without.

Your Personal Leadership Assessment

Are you an effective leader? The answer depends on how well and consistently you:

1. Communicate

   • Can you explain your vision so that others will understand you and want to follow you?

   • Are you credible? People will follow a leader they trust even if they're not quite certain where they're headed. It's important to communicate your goals to those who will be able to help you. Equally important is your ability to demonstrate your trustworthiness and your willingness to put your trust in those you wish to lead.

2. Motivate

   • Do you treat people with respect? For example, do you:

     ☐ Understand what is important to them?

     ☐ Recognize their strengths and drawbacks?

     ☐ Give *specific* feedback on performance?

     ☐ Help them develop the personal and professional skills they need to succeed?

Many people will follow a leader who has demonstrated aggressiveness, but more people will follow a leader who knows how to motivate through a combination of strength, intellect, and fairness.

3. Inspire

   • Are you accessible and available to share your ideas, insights, and experiences with the members of your team?

   • In today's business environment, there is more diversity among employees than ever. Do you recognize and appreciate each of your employee's particular skills, talents, and contributions? Do you make a special effort to ensure that all members of the team feel valued and worthwhile?

Exercise 5

RECOGNIZING THE LEADERS IN YOUR ORGANIZATION

You've just learned what it takes to be a leader. Now, take this information and apply it to the people you know within your own organization. Who are the people that you, as a Promotable Person, should choose to be your role models and your mentors? Who are the people who can best help you develop your own leadership skills and potential?

Answer the following questions to help you identify the leaders within your organization.

1. Who do people go to for advice? _____

_____

2. Who speaks well of his or her employees? _____

_____

3. Who takes risks that usually pay off? _____

_____

4. Who gets assigned to "plum" tasks (you know, the high-visibility jobs that everyone wants, but only a chosen few get)? _____

_____

5. Who has the charisma that makes people naturally want to imitate or follow them? _____

_____

6. Whose ideas are respected and implemented? _____

_____

7. Who is getting promoted? _____

_____

Once you have identified the people in Exercise 5, get to know them. Watch them. Work with them whenever possible. And, above all, always keep your eyes, ears, and mind open when you're around them. What you learn could take you a long way toward being a more Promotable Person.

APPLYING LEADERSHIP TRAITS

The twelve traits leaders commonly share helps them to be effective in these three important areas:

- Problem solving and decision making

- Team building

- Delegating

Problem Solving and Decision Making

Within every organization, problems arise and decisions must be made. Somebody has to take the initiative to solve the problems and make the decisions. That takes a leader.

When faced with a problem, remember, first of all, not to panic. Think about the problem logically. Plan how you will proceed toward a favorable conclusion. Don't hesitate to ask for input from others. You can always learn from other people's experience and ideas.

As you formulate your plans, keep these seven suggestions in mind:

1. Avoid acting hastily, if at all possible.

2. Define what the problem is and write it down.

3. Organize and evaluate all available, relevant information.

4. Ask questions, collect data, and extend your reach beyond what you already know.

5. Develop a list of alternative solutions. Next to each solution, make a column marked "Pros" and one marked "Cons" and list the advantages and disadvantages of that solution. (See the Problem-Solving/Decision-Making Worksheet on page 32.)

6. Analyze each solution in terms of its pros and cons. Make comparisons.

7. Choose the decision that best solves the problem.

Effective leaders realize that problems are a part of everyday work life. Because they expect to encounter problems, they are not usually overwhelmed by them when they occur. They are able to keep their heads and think through logical, workable solutions.

But being a leader doesn't mean you have to solve *everyone's* problems all the time. As a leader you must be able—and willing—to empower the members of your team to make their own decisions and solve their own problems whenever possible and appropriate.

Exercise 6

PROBLEM-SOLVING/ DECISION-MAKING WORKSHEET

Consider a problem you're currently facing. Use the space below to define the problem, to weigh the pros and cons of possible solutions, and finally to choose a solution.

Define Problem: _____

_____

_____

_____

_____

_____

Solutions	**Pros**	**Cons**
1. _____	_____	_____
_____	_____	_____
2. _____	_____	_____
_____	_____	_____
3. _____	_____	_____
_____	_____	_____
4. _____	_____	_____
_____	_____	_____
5. _____	_____	_____
_____	_____	_____
6. _____	_____	_____
_____	_____	_____

7. _____   _____   _____

   _____   _____   _____

8. _____   _____   _____

   _____   _____   _____

Solution Chosen: _____

_____

_____

_____

_____

_____

The Importance of Team Development

No man—or woman—is an island. Not even the Promotable Person. A good leader recognizes the necessity and value of support, of a team made up of employees working together toward a single goal.

Strong teams don't just happen. They must be built. And they must constantly be reinforced so they don't fall apart under pressure or strain. That's why one of your most important functions as a leader is to foster a spirit of unity and teamwork among your employees.

Members of a team need to feel a close connection to their leader. So it is important that you, as the leader, make yourself accessible to them on a regular basis.

Team members must feel confident that their leader can provide guidance and sound counsel when they need it. It is also up to the leader to make sure that each member feels valued and important, both as an individual and as part of the team.

As the leader, you must know when—and how—to give recognition to your team members. You must know when that recognition should spotlight a particular individual and when it should focus on the efforts of the entire team.

But leadership isn't all praise and cheerleading. It also requires the ability to offer constructive criticism without demoralizing your team members or making them feel overly defensive.

The leader must set the standard for the team. If you demonstrate a strong commitment to give your best, the other team members will be inspired to give their best. Remember, the strongest leaders are the ones who lead by example.

Delegating for Success

Working hard doesn't necessarily make you a leader. Working smart does. A true leader understands that the important thing is to get the job done in the most efficient and effective way. Many times that means delegating work to others.

The ability to delegate is crucial for the Promotable Person. However, some people hesitate to delegate for a variety of reasons. They may be afraid that people will think they can't handle their workload. They may not want to take the time to explain the job to someone else. Or they may truly believe that no one can do the job better than they can themselves.

In reality, delegating can be a real time-saver. Even more important, it can be a life-saver (see Chapter 5, which discusses how stress can be a power robber). And it really is easy, once you get the hang of it. Just follow these basic steps:

1. Make sure *you* know exactly what you want done.

2. Decide whether the task can be delegated.

3. Determine who is best qualified to do the job.

4. Give clear instructions.

5. Be specific about deadlines, format, parameters, and other details. (Put your expectations in writing, if necessary.)

6. Evaluate and give feedback.

No matter how much of a hurry you may be in, it's never fair to just dump a job on someone's desk and expect that person to "figure it out." His or her interpretation of what needs to be done may be very different from yours. And instead of saving a little time by skipping the explanation, you may find yourself spending hours redoing the work later.

Once you learn to delegate effectively, you'll find your productivity level increasing along with your employees' competence—and confidence. Your ability to delegate will clearly demonstrate your skill as a professional, a leader, and as a Promotable Person who can handle a heavy workload.

That's exactly what Susan Ferris, a midlevel manager in a pharmaceutical firm, learned after she was told during a performance appraisal that she appeared to be overwhelmed by her workload. This feedback made Susan realize that by doing all the work herself, she was neither utilizing the expertise available to her nor was she empowering others in her group. Even worse was the undeniable fact that she was burning herself out.

Although it was difficult at first, she slowly began to delegate and was pleasantly surprised to realize that the quality of work was maintained, her employees were growing in their jobs and, most important of all, she no longer felt overwhelmed. As time passed, Susan found it easier and easier to delegate. She now delegates regularly—and effectively. In fact, her latest performance appraisal was proof of just how effective she has become: she was promoted.

Promotable Assignments

1. Identify the leaders in your organization. Analyze your relationships with them. Find ways to build them into your network.

2. Evaluate your leadership qualities by answering the questions under "Your Personal Leadership Assessment" on page 28. Identify where you need to grow.

▲ CHAPTER 4

Become an Expert

Every person is particularly knowledgeable or skilled in a certain area. The Promotable Person understands the importance of using that knowledge and skill to establish an area of expertise—and of making sure that others recognize that expertise.

An expert is someone who stays current with changes occurring in his or her field. That means there's never time to just rest in yesterday's achievements. Even if you're an expert today, you have to keep learning and growing. If you don't, be assured that you won't remain an expert for long.

True expertise reflects a commitment to excellence. It shows you care enough to be the best at what you do. In a world where so many people are satisfied to settle for mediocrity, it's no wonder that the expert commands so much respect—and gets so many promotions.

THE **EXPERT** SELF-DEVELOPMENT MODEL

What really makes a person an expert? Even more important, how can you become one? You can start by following this model:

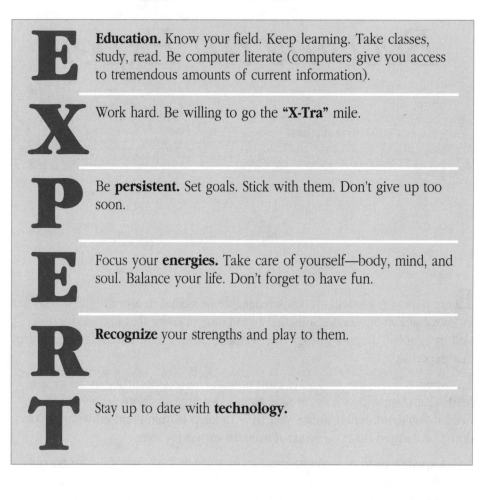

Education. Know your field. Keep learning. Take classes, study, read. Be computer literate (computers give you access to tremendous amounts of current information).

Work hard. Be willing to go the **"X-Tra"** mile.

Be **persistent.** Set goals. Stick with them. Don't give up too soon.

Focus your **energies.** Take care of yourself—body, mind, and soul. Balance your life. Don't forget to have fun.

Recognize your strengths and play to them.

Stay up to date with **technology.**

Of course, everyone can point to instances where people have been promoted for reasons that had little or nothing to do with their skills and knowledge. These reasons may have involved politics, timing, or just plain good luck. However, you can't control these things—and you certainly can't count on them.

Instead of wishing and waiting to be promoted, put your energies where they'll do the most good. Develop your own area of expertise. Take steps to get yourself recognized. Make yourself known and you'll make yourself promotable.

That's what John did. A university graduate who majored in computers, John was hired as a programmer by a major bank. His passion and curiosity about the rapidly developing computer field drove him to learn everything he could about computers. As he studied, he realized that PCs would be the future of business.

He also volunteered on teams to convert his organization's systems to PCs. He took additional classes at night to learn about the newest software.

Through his efforts, John's company saved millions of dollars, and John was promoted to manager of his department. He is also in high demand as a speaker on computer technology issues. And he is still as passionate and as curious about computers as ever.

John is a true expert. Are you? If you're not yet, what are you doing to become one? Answer "yes" or "no" to the following questions to assess your progress.

Exercise 7

SELF-ASSESSMENT: AM I DEVELOPING AN AREA OF EXPERTISE?

	Yes	No
1. Are you a member of your professional organization?	☐	☐
2. Do you subscribe to journals and newsletters in your field?	☐	☐
3. Do you attend workshops, seminars, and classes that focus on your field or other related topics?	☐	☐
4. Do you give presentations on topics that pertain to your field?	☐	☐
5. Do you seek out other experts?	☐	☐
6. Do you read your organization's annual report?	☐	☐
7. Do you volunteer to work on cross-departmental activities?	☐	☐
8. Do you keep up with trends in your industry or developments that might have an impact on your industry?	☐	☐
9. Do you have a professional network?	☐	☐
10. Do you ask for feedback on the quality of your work?	☐	☐

Undoubtedly, you already realize you should have answered "yes" to all of these questions. If you didn't, you know what you have to do. Make a plan. Put it into action. Then go over the self-assessment again and again until every "no" becomes a "yes."

MAKING A CHANGE

Being an acknowledged expert in your current job doesn't mean you can't ever move out of that job. But you may be concerned that if you do, you'll lose all the status and respect you have worked so hard to earn. Well, relax. You can use the same skills that made you an expert in your current job to establish yourself in your new job. Here are some tips to make your transition easier and smoother:

- Talk to people in the field or fields that may be of interest to you.

- Know the basic educational requirements for a position in the field of your choice. Will you need a bachelor's degree? a master's? a doctorate?

- Study the field. Take courses. Read up.

- Join professional organizations and volunteer for committees.

- Don't minimize your capabilities and knowledge when discussing your interest in a position in another field.

- Be focused. Set goals.

- Be positive. Expect the best and you're more likely to get it.

- Once you make the move, become an expert in your new field.

For the true expert, the personal growth and satisfaction that come with doing an outstanding job are rewards in and of themselves. The professional rewards—including recognition and respect—are bonuses. And, then, of course, there's the biggest bonus of all. It is the career advancement that comes with expertise—the ultimate reward for the Promotable Person.

Promotable Assignments

1. Analyze what new developments or changes are happening in your field. Sign up for a course in that area.

2. Look for an opportunity—either in your organization or in your professional association—to make a presentation in your area of expertise.

▲ CHAPTER 5

The Power Robbers

Power. If only you had it, nothing could stop you from achieving your personal and career goals.

The fact is, you already have all the power you need to control your life—and your promotability. But it's up to you to develop and direct this power. It's also up to you to protect it from the forces that would steal it away from you: the *power robbers*.

The power robbers are sneaky. You can't see them. But if you're not constantly on guard against them, they can sabotage your promotability. They can divert your energy, decrease your productivity, and undermine your professional effectiveness—if you let them.

Fortunately, it isn't difficult to defend yourself against the power robbers once you know what they are and how they work. Here are the three most common power robbers:

- Lack of time management

- Inability to control stress

- Fear of risk-taking

This chapter will help you determine whether the power robbers are stalling your career. It also contains specific steps you can take to protect the tremendous personal power you have at your command and to use that power to enhance your status as a Promotable Person.

POWER ROBBER #1: LACK OF TIME MANAGEMENT

Each day is twenty-four hours long. It's the same for everyone, no exceptions. Then why is it that some people are able to get so much more accomplished than others during that twenty-four-hour period? The answer is time management.

Being able to manage time effectively is one of the most important skills that separates the Promotable Person from the average employee. Are your time management skills helping or hindering your promotability? Take the time management self-assessment that follows to find out.

Exercise 8

CAN *I* IMPROVE *MY* TIME MANAGEMENT SKILLS?

Answer the following questions "yes" or "no."

	Yes	No
1. I use a daily planning sheet.	☐	☐
2. I prioritize my activities.	☐	☐
3. I don't put off doing tasks that are difficult or unpleasant.	☐	☐
4. At meetings, I use an agenda.	☐	☐
5. I show that I value others' time by keeping telephone conversations brief and to the point.	☐	☐
6. I can accurately estimate the time I need to complete tasks.	☐	☐
7. I effectively use "waiting time" (e.g., time spent waiting for meetings to begin, time spent in the car, etc.).	☐	☐
8. I usually set realistic deadlines for myself.	☐	☐
9. I break large or complicated jobs into manageable pieces and then tackle the job one piece at a time.	☐	☐
10. I know when and how to delegate responsibility.	☐	☐

If you answered "no" to all or most of these statements, chances are your lack of time management skills is jeopardizing your professional effectiveness and status as a Promotable Person. Although most of us were raised to believe that putting in long, hard hours was the key to success, that isn't necessarily the case in today's business world. In fact, as the following example illustrates, just the opposite may be true.

John, the senior project manager at ABC Company, regularly puts in extra hours to get his job done. It is not at all unusual for him to remain at his desk far into the night.

His boss, the vice president, recognizes that John always gets his job done. But he believes that many of the extra hours John spends working are unnecessary and, even worse, are the result of John's inability to effectively manage his time.

For instance, the vice president notices that John isn't organized. He doesn't prioritize his tasks and always seems to be scrambling to meet some immediate deadline. John also spends a lot of time socializing with his co-workers, a habit that disrupts not only his own work but also distracts everyone on the project.

John thinks he is doing an excellent job because he has never missed an important deadline. Yet when a higher level position opens up, he is passed over—again. And he will continue to be passed over as long as his lack of time management skills keeps him off the vice president's list of promotable candidates.

As John's story demonstrates, it's not necessarily the person who works the most hours who makes it to the top of the corporate ladder. Rather, it's the person who knows how to make the most out of every hour he or she works.

Time Management Problems

Take a moment to look back at your own time management self-assessment. Look specifically at the questions you answered "no" to. See whether you can categorize your time management problems under one of these four general headings:

- Poor planning

- Inability to say "no"

- Procrastination

- Poor work habits

Poor planning. If you often feel that you're being pulled in ten different directions at once or if the deadlines you're expected to meet often seem overwhelming, the problem may not be your job. It may be your inability to organize your tasks.

The Promotable Person knows that a little planning can go a long way. In fact, planning can make the difference between controlling your job—and allowing your job to control you.

Your first reaction to all this might be, "Who has time to plan when I barely have time to finish the work I already have?" Well, that's just the point. The fact is, a little planning can end up saving you a lot of time.

For example, say you are given a big, complicated project to do. At first, the job may seem so overwhelming that you don't even know where to start. You could take a deep breath and just jump in anywhere. Or you could take a few moments to plan out your approach to the project in this way:

1. Take a look at the project as a whole.

2. Break it up into smaller, more manageable pieces.

3. Assign the specific tasks necessary to complete each piece.

4. Prioritize the tasks.

5. Set realistic deadlines.

6. Work on the tasks in order of their priority.

Having the right planning tools can also be a major time-saver. But only if you get into the habit of using them regularly. Whether you prefer to work manually or on a computer, there are a number of time management tools designed to make your days more efficient and your life easier.

Another benefit of planning is that it gives you an opportunity to determine whether your expectations are realistic or whether you're taking on too much at one time. Once you have organized and prioritized your tasks and set your deadlines, take a moment to think about whether the workload, timelines, and expectations are realistic.

For example, if you know that it will probably take you two weeks to do the research necessary for the project, don't assign yourself a deadline of one week. Or if you know you have three other major deadlines on a particular day, try to avoid setting another one for that same day. Of course, in business, as in every aspect of life, sometimes things happen that you can't control. But planning can help you avoid making these emergency situations an everyday occurrence.

Inability to say "no." It's only natural to want your co-workers to like or respect you. And you've always understood that being regarded as a "team player" is important to your promotability. So when you're asked to help out by taking on some extra work, how can you possibly refuse?

While it's important to consider yourself as part of a team working toward a singular goal, it's just as important to recognize how you can make the strongest contribution to the team and to focus your time and energy on those strengths. Sometimes that means saying "no" to a job that doesn't fall into your area of responsibility or expertise. It may also mean saying "no" to adding another deadline to your already full schedule.

Procrastination. You come into work in the morning, sit down at your desk, pull out your daily schedule, and read off the first task you've designated for the day. Oh no, not that! You're not in the mood to tackle anything that difficult this morning. Maybe it would be better to put that task off until later in the afternoon or, better yet, until tomorrow...

Watch out! You're about to walk right into one of *the* most dangerous time-stealing traps. Think about it. Each day you put off one or two tasks that just seem too time-consuming, difficult, or unpleasant to tackle at the time. And each morning, you find new reasons why you have to put off working on those tasks for just one more day. Then, one morning, you find yourself faced with a schedule filled with time-consuming, difficult, or unpleasant tasks that can't be put off one day longer because they're all on deadline. Scary prospect, isn't it?

Poor work habits. You're twenty minutes late to work again. Then, you spend ten more minutes shuffling through the piles of papers on your overloaded desk searching for the document your boss wants *immediately*. Then it's time for morning coffee—and a half-hour chat about your weekend plans with your co-workers. A few minutes here, a few minutes there. Before you know it, you've already lost an hour out of your workday.

That's not just bad news for your employer. It's bad news for you, too, because you're the one who is going to have to make up that hour—somehow, sometime. And poor work habits do more than steal your time. They also undermine your professional image.

Some poor work habits are obvious: the messy desk, chronic lateness, sloppy note-taking or total lack of note-taking, excessive socializing during working hours, unnecessarily long phone calls—the list goes on. But did you ever stop to think about how much time you spend each day just waiting—in reception areas for appointments? in cars, planes, and trains? for meetings to begin or phone calls to be returned? Do you use this time productively, or do you allow "wait time" to become "waste time?"

Ten Tips for Effective Time Management

1. Before you can begin to manage your time, you have to decide to manage your time. It doesn't just happen, but it is within your control.

2. Use proper planning tools. Here are some of them:

- A daily planning sheet or "To Do" list (see sample on page 51).

- A calendar (an at-a-glance reference for meetings, deadlines, etc.).

- Computer time management software.

- A master schedule of long-term goals.

3. Schedule daily planning time. At the beginning or end of each day, take ten minutes to create a daily "To Do" list. On Monday mornings, take twenty minutes to create a schedule for the entire week.

4. Prioritize. The Promotable Person always thinks of the big picture as well as the individual tasks at hand. Keep long-term goals in mind when setting immediate priorities. How you prioritize projects and tasks depends on a number of variables, including external deadlines, politics, visibility (yours and your boss's), and the impact on the bottom line. Your priorities should be in concert with those of your organization and your boss. It's not enough to do only the things that are easy and fun for you. In fact, the Promotable Person views tackling difficult tasks as a personal challenge and as an opportunity to present a professional image.

5. Control interruptions. A co-worker stops by your office for a mid-afternoon chat. Your friend calls to catch up on plans for the weekend. It's often difficult to tell people you like that you don't have time to talk to them. Fortunately, if you follow these tips, you can let them know with a minimum amount of damage to their feelings and to your relationships:

Office visitors

- Set time limits right from the start. For example, saying "I have my next meeting in twenty minutes" lets the visitor know you are on a definite schedule.

- Close your door. This is a clear indication to others that you are busy and do not wish to be interrupted.

Sample Daily Planning Sheet/"To Do" List

	Things To Do	**Time Required**	**Priority Rank**
1.			
2.			
3.			
4.			
5.			
6.			
7.			
8.			
9.			
10.			

To get even more mileage out of this Daily "To Do" List, use it in conjunction with a daily appointment page. First, plug in any meetings or appointments you have for the day. Then, beginning with your highest priority, block out chunks of time for completing each of the tasks on your "To Do" list. In this way, you're setting specific appointments with yourself throughout the day to tackle the items on your "To Do" list.

- Stand up to indicate when your meeting is over. This firm, yet polite signal is usually impossible to misunderstand or ignore.

Telephone calls

- Keep chatty personal or social calls to a minimum.

- Set time limits. For example, at the beginning of the conversation, ask the caller, "How much time will this take?"

- Learn to terminate conversations. Statements such as "I have a deadline to meet, so we'll have to wrap this up in five minutes" lets the caller know you have to get back to work and minimizes the possibility of bruised egos.

6. **Learn to delegate.** We've all heard the saying, "If you want a job done right, do it yourself." Well, if you want to be a Promotable Person, that's one bit of advice you'll ignore.

Forget the notion that delegating is just another word for "passing the buck." One of the most important skills today's Promotable Person must develop is the ability to delegate tasks and responsibilities. The willingness to delegate is not a weakness. Quite the opposite. It's a strength that characterizes the most effective and most successful executives.

In fact, the higher you go up the corporate ladder and the more your responsibilities increase, the more you'll have to delegate. After all, why do you think your boss hired you?

Delegating isn't something that comes naturally to most people. Many times, it just seems easier and quicker to do a job yourself rather than take the time and effort to train someone else to do it and then to monitor whether the job actually gets done. That may be true for the short run. But in the long run, however, effective delegating can actually save you a great deal of time and aggravation.

Here are some tips for delegating effectively:

- Review your list of tasks one by one and ask yourself: "Do I have to do this myself or can someone else do it?" Sometimes you may realize that the task doesn't need to be done at all!

- Choose the right person for the job. Don't set yourself up to be aggravated by assigning a job to someone who may not have the skills or knowledge to handle it.

- Take the time to explain the job and set a deadline. Don't expect people to read your mind.

7. **Know your own time clock.** Some people get up in the morning fresh, alert, and raring to go. Others take a little longer to get their engines revved into full gear. We all have our own internal clocks that tell us what time of day is most productive for us.

Instead of trying to fight your time clock, learn to work with it. Whenever possible, schedule your daily tasks to coincide with and make the most of your peak hours. For instance, if you're a morning person, try to schedule your most challenging tasks early in the day. Save less demanding activities such as reading the mail for the afternoon.

Make sure to schedule in some time for rest each day. Both your body and your mind need some time to relax and recharge or you risk mental and physical burnout. (For some relaxation techniques, see "Power Robber #2: Inability to Control Stress," which begins on page 55.)

8. **Manage your paper.** Avoid paper clutter. You save time in two ways: you don't have to handle the paper itself more than once and you don't have to spend time looking through a cluttered desk to find the things you need. Here are some paper-handling tips:

- Set up a good, well-labeled filing system and use it.

- If at all possible, don't put a piece of paper down without deciding what you're going to do with it. For example, after reading a letter, decide whether it requires an answer or should be filed for reference. If an answer is required, do it as soon as possible. Often, you can jot down the reply on the same piece of paper the memo or letter is printed on.

- Learn to skim when reading. You'll be amazed at how much more quickly you can speed through your mail.

9. **Use your waiting time creatively.** No matter what you do, no matter how well you plan, you just can't avoid it: waiting time.

Waiting is a fact of life. And, unfortunately, you can't always control other people's schedules or their manners. But there is one important thing you can control about waiting time. How you use it.

Always be prepared to wait. When you go out for an appointment, take along some reading material or other work. That way, instead of sitting and tapping your foot when you find yourself "on hold" in someone's reception area, you can take care of your mail or read that interesting article you clipped from a business magazine.

Keep some instructional or motivational tapes in your car. Listening to tapes is much more productive—and less nerve-wracking—than just sitting and stewing in the middle of a traffic jam.

10. **Above all, be realistic and flexible.** You have two choices. You can either be a reactive person—a person to whom things happen. Or you can be a proactive person—a person who makes things happen. For the Promotable Person, the choice is clear.

Keep in mind, however, that it's not necessary to be a superhero. If your schedule or expectations of yourself aren't realistic, you'll only set yourself up to fail.

The best guideline is this: Don't make promises you can't keep. Don't set deadlines you know you can't meet. Record how much time it actually takes to accomplish tasks so you can be more accurate in your scheduling.

Even the best-laid plans can go awry for any number of reasons. Crises do arise. The Promotable Person understands that in order to do business in the real world, organization must be tempered by flexibility. In other words, you have to learn to roll with the punches. That's why the Promotable Person deliberately *schedules* free time for crisis management.

POWER ROBBER #2: INABILITY TO CONTROL STRESS

Lack of time management is a major contributor to stress, but it's not the only one. There are any number of stressors that can affect the way we live and work. Which stressors affect you the most? Take the stress self-assessment in Exercise 9 to find out.

Good and Bad Stress

Let's face it, stress is all around us. It's part of our daily lives. But while it's impossible for anyone to totally avoid stress, the Promotable Person is able to recognize and manage it before it gets out of hand.

Before you can learn to manage stress, you have to understand it. And that begins with defining it. Exactly what is stress? Quite simply, it's our reaction to life.

Contrary to popular belief, not all stress is bad. In fact, it can even be quite positive. A certain amount of stress can drive you to work harder, faster, and better. It can be that extra push that enables you to meet challenges and create opportunities.

Problems can begin when stress is prolonged. Over time, mental and physical strain can build up. Excitement turns to tension. Instead of being stimulated, you feel drained. Too much stress can threaten your health. Ultimately, it can even kill you.

The Promotable Person knows how to harness the power of good stress without falling victim to bad stress. But first, it's important to recognize that there's a fine line between drive and overdrive. The key to stress management is striking a personal balance. Here are some techniques to help you manage your stress and achieve that crucial balance in your life. Practice these guidelines *daily* to help you relax.

1. **Breathe.** When you feel bad stress building, slowly breathe in through your nose, tighten the muscles in your body, hold your breath for a count of six, and then slowly release the tension. Repeat this process until you begin to feel more relaxed and in control.

Exercise 9

IDENTIFYING STRESSORS THAT MOST AFFECT ME

The following is a list of common stressors. Check all that apply to you, both at work and at home.

☐ 1. Inability to complete tasks

☐ 2. Too many things to do in a day

☐ 3. Inadequate preparation for job

☐ 4. Lack of privacy

☐ 5. Unrealistic expectations

☐ 6. Undefined expectations or job responsibilities

☐ 7. Information overload

☐ 8. Too little authority

☐ 9. Sexual harassment

☐ 10. Change in work or personal life

☐ 11. Lack of job security

☐ 12. Marital problems

☐ 13. Recent move

☐ 14. Serious illness

☐ 15. Problems with children

☐ 16. Long work commute

☐ 17. Problems with co-workers

☐ 18. Need for perfection, from yourself or from others

If simply taking this quiz has caused your anxiety level to rise, you're in real need of some immediate stress management. Follow the guidelines in this chapter to reduce your stress level.

2. Schedule in some downtime. Find a few a minutes each day for activities you enjoy:

- Read ten pages of a novel.

- Spend time working with a hobby or playing your favorite sport.

- Take a long, hot bath.

- Listen to relaxation tapes.

3. Exercise. It's no secret that exercise is good for your body. Many medical authorities also agree that it's the number one defense against stress. But for many people, the whole issue becomes a Catch-22. How can exercise help control stress when just thinking about squeezing it into your already overloaded schedule causes your anxiety level to soar? The solution is to think about exercise creatively:

- Park your car as far away from the front door as possible and walk.

- Take the steps instead of the elevator whenever possible.

- Take a walk at lunch.

4. Get a good night's sleep. Establish and stick to a regular bedtime. Remember, too, not to eat or drink anything with caffeine within at least four hours of bedtime. Above all, keep your briefcase out of the bedroom. That means no paperwork in bed.

5. Eat a balanced diet. Schedule time for meals, and don't skip breakfast or lunch. Many people fall into the habit of turning to the coffee or candy machine for energy. Don't. Caffeine and sugar may give you an initial "rush" of energy, but it's short-lived. Often, once this high wears off, you feel even more tired than before. Keep a piece of fruit in your desk for emergency snacking.

6. Pray or meditate. You can't control everything all the time. Learn to let go and give yourself a break.

7. Use imagery. Focus on the positive instead of the negative. Mentally transport yourself to someplace peaceful and free of stress (e.g., a quiet beach, your garden, etc.)

8. **Be assertive.** Learn to express your ideas and point of view in a calm, positive, noncombative manner. Sometimes, this means learning to say "no."

9. **Delegate.** Follow this advice at home as well as at work. Get the family involved in housework and errands. If you need it and can afford it, hire help.

10. **Let go of perfection.** Striving for excellence is admirable. But always keep in mind that nobody's expected to be perfect, including you. Mistakes are a part of life. They can also be valuable learning experiences.

11. **Don't forget to pamper yourself once in a while.** You work hard. Reward yourself with something that's special to you. Have a massage, take a vacation, go out to dinner. Enjoy—you deserve it!

POWER ROBBER #3: FEAR OF RISK-TAKING

Risk-takers are the people who get ahead. On the other hand, risk-takers are also the people who get fired.

The Promotable Person is a risk-taker. But every risk is calculated, the pros and cons are considered, the potential problems and rewards are weighed. Although risk-taking comes with no guarantees, The Promotable Person knows how to identify real opportunities and is not afraid to go for them.

Playing it safe is comfortable. It can also stagnate you and your career. Without risk-taking, there is no growth.

Studies have confirmed that risk-takers are the people who are most likely to rise up the corporate ladder. The most successful are those who have helpful bosses who encourage risk-taking.

Of course, it's easy to say, "Just get out there and do it—take the risk." That would be like blindfolding someone, leading him or her to the edge of a cliff, and saying, "Just go on and jump." The Promotable Person is courageous, not foolhardy. Before deciding to take a risk, the Promotable Person:

- Is clear about what he or she wants.
- Seeks out advice from trusted mentors.
- Evaluates the pros and cons of the situation.
- Weighs the consequences of not taking the risk.
- Confronts fears.
- Knows personal limitations.
- Is able to learn from his or her bosses and move on.
- Listens to gut feelings.

Most of all, the Promotable Person is someone who is willing to accept the consequences for decisions and actions—a trait that truly differentiates a leader from a follower and a run-of-the-mill employee from a Promotable Person.

Consider this example:

> A young supervisor at a major pharmaceutical firm shocked his co-workers at an open forum meeting with a company vice president by presenting what many considered to be an extreme recommendation for changing a process at the company's bottling plant. The buzz among the supervisor's co-workers was that this rash action was sure to get him fired. But just the reverse occurred. Instead of being fired, the young supervisor was promoted to assistant plant manager within one year after his plan was implemented!

> So what happens if you take a risk and things don't work out exactly as you had planned? You could dwell on it, brood on it, and let it teach you a lesson never to take another risk. Or you could prove that you know how to evaluate the situation, learn from it, and move on. Above all, don't allow yourself to become discouraged. No one's perfect (no, not even you). And who knows? Your next calculated risk could be your springboard to promotion.

PROMOTABLE ASSIGNMENTS

1. Next Monday morning, *start getting organized.* Set aside twenty minutes to plan your week—no excuses.

2. Spend one hour sometime during the next week in personal relaxation or exercise. You deserve it, so give yourself permission.

3. Take a calculated risk—a small one to get started. Evaluate your actions before, during, and after. Don't be discouraged, no matter what the outcome.

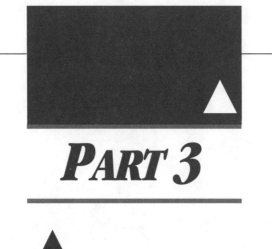

PART 3

Communicating
With Others

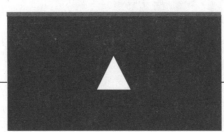

▲ CHAPTER 6

Developing Your Writing and Speaking Skills

You have the technical expertise. And you have a million great ideas. But it's not enough to merely think brilliant thoughts. The Promotable Person must also be able to effectively express those thoughts to others.

A recent survey revealed that lack of crucial communication skills accounts for 80 percent of the reason why people don't get promoted. Many people actually turn down job promotions because they are afraid their writing and speaking skills won't measure up to those required in higher-level positions.

Every business letter you write, every presentation you deliver is an opportunity to demonstrate your competence and your professionalism—in short, your "promotability." But you don't have to possess the writing skills of a Pulitzer Prize-winning author or the speaking skills of a great orator to talk your way up the corporate ladder. All you need is the ability to get your ideas across clearly and with confidence.

Easier said than done? Not really. In this chapter, you will find many tips and techniques for strengthening your writing and speaking skills. You may be surprised at how simple many of these techniques are. But don't be fooled by their simplicity. They are your key to harnessing one of the greatest sources of power in today's business world—the power of the written and spoken word.

Exercise 10

GETTING OUT THE WORD

The Promotable Person is one who is equally adept at communicating orally and on paper. Answer "true" or "false" to each question in the following self-assessment to find out whether you have the communications skills you need to get ahead.

	True	False
A. When writing, I:		
1. Keep my reader in mind.	☐	☐
2. State clearly the purpose of my correspondence.	☐	☐
3. Use the appropriate salutation.	☐	☐
4. Start with a strong opening sentence.	☐	☐
5. Use simple and clear language.	☐	☐
6. Avoid jargon and buzzwords.	☐	☐
7. Provide facts and details to support my main points.	☐	☐
8. Use short sentences.	☐	☐
9. Read my writing out loud. (You can spot your mistakes more easily this way.)	☐	☐
10. Carefully proofread my documents before sending them.	☐	☐

	True	**False**

B. When preparing an oral presentation, I:

1. Have a clear understanding of the purpose of my presentation. ☐ ☐

2. Analyze my audience before preparing my presentation. ☐ ☐

3. Organize my presentation with the audience viewpoint in mind. ☐ ☐

4. Start with a strong opening. ☐ ☐

5. Use language that my audience understands. ☐ ☐

6. Look for ways to prevent my presentation from being a "data dump" of facts and figures. ☐ ☐

7. Use humor appropriately. ☐ ☐

8. End by drawing conclusions. ☐ ☐

9. Practice my presentation out loud. ☐ ☐

10. Manage my stage fright. ☐ ☐

If you answered "true" to all or most of these statements, you are probably a polished communicator with excellent career potential. If you answered "false" to many of the statements, don't panic. Help is on the way.

STRENGTHENING YOUR WRITING SKILLS

For many people, nothing is more intimidating than a blank sheet of paper. Whether it's a report, a business letter, or even a simple thank-you note, any project can seem as daunting as trying to write *War and Peace* if you can't think of how to begin, what to say, or how to say it.

No matter what you are writing, whether it is a report, business letter, memo, fax, or even e-mail, there are five basic steps you should always keep in mind.

1. **Keep it short.** For a letter or memo, one page is usually enough. E-mail can be even shorter. Use short paragraphs and sentences, eliminating extra words. In other words, say what you have to say and stop!

2. **Define your purpose.** Don't meander, ramble, or bury your purpose under superfluous language or preliminary detail. Think about the main points you want to get across to your reader, and make them as quickly as possible.

3. **Write the way you speak.** You want to connect with your reader just as if you were having a one-on-one conversation. In the past, "proper" business writing was much more stilted. Today, that same writing would sound stuffy, perhaps even pompous. So don't overthink your writing. Just be yourself.

4. **Use simple and clear language.** Don't make your reader work to understand what you're trying to say. Avoid big words and flowery language. They can be distracting and even annoying to the reader. If you want to impress your reader, choose words that will make your point most clearly and powerfully.

5. **Read your documents out loud.** *Listen to the language.* Does it flow in your natural conversational voice? Or does it sound stilted? *Listen to the content.* Are the main points of the document easy to identify? Are they easy to understand? Will your readers be able to recognize what action you plan to take or what action you are asking them to take? *Check the spelling and punctuation.* When you read something over silently, you can easily gloss over misspellings, typos, and missing words and letters. You can also overlook missed or misplaced punctuation marks. Reading aloud requires a slower pace and closer attention to each word, making it easier to spot errors. *Read your document in hard copy.* It's easier to catch your mistakes on paper than on a computer screen. You can also catch spacing problems that may not appear on the screen.

The Art and Craft of Writing Business Letters

Ever wonder why it's sometimes so hard to begin to write business letters? Many times it's because you haven't given yourself a chance to sufficiently organize your thoughts.

When it comes to drafting a letter, a little advance preparation can save you good writing—and rewriting—time. It will also help you produce a document that is clear, powerful, and effective.

The first step, of course, is to identify your reader. Is it your boss? A colleague? A customer? Then put yourself in that reader's shoes. Remember, people pay attention and respond most strongly to things that pertain to them personally. Keep this in mind at all times while you are composing your letter.

Every business letter has these five major components:

1. **Salutation.** Be sure to use the person's correct name and title. Don't address the recipient by his or her first name unless you are certain it is acceptable to do so. If you don't know the recipient's gender, use both the first and last name. For example, you would write "Dear Pat Smith" instead of "Dear Mr. Smith" or "Dear Ms. Smith." If you don't know the recipient's name, use a nongender-specific, nonsexist term such as "Dear Client" or "Dear ABC Company Representative."

2. **Beginning.** Your opening paragraph should clearly state the purpose or topic of your letter.

3. **Middle.** Support your opening statement with pertinent details, facts, and descriptions.

4. **End.** What action do you plan to take or do you want the reader to take? This part of the letter is extremely important. If you don't include a plan of action or call to action, you may leave the reader feeling confused or apathetic.

5. Complimentary closing. Your choice of closings will depend on the level of familiarity you have with the reader and the formality of the tone you wish to establish. For instance, "Respectfully" and "Respectfully yours" are extremely formal closings, usually reserved for correspondence with government officials or members of the clergy. "Sincerely" and "Sincerely yours" are frequently used for business contacts. "Best regards" and "Cordially" may be used when you know the reader well and the tone of your letter is informal.

A Few Words of Thanks

"Thank you" has to be one of the most underused phrases in business. That's surprising because it doesn't take much time and effort—and it always elicits a positive reaction.

When you go out of your way for someone, don't you like your extra effort to be acknowledged? Everyone does. A thank-you note is a gesture of respect, a way of saying "I value your time, effort, and support." Even the busiest corporate head has time to enjoy a little appreciation.

But in today's hectic business world, it's easy to find excuses not to write thank-you notes. "I'm too busy" is a common explanation. "No one takes the time to read them anyway" is another. Well, the answer to both those excuses is wrong and wrong.

The Promotable Person is never too busy to take a few minutes to jot down a few well-chosen words of thanks to a supervisor, colleague, or customer. Each note takes only a few minutes to write, yet the return on that time can be immeasurable in terms of enhancing your image as a competent, thoughtful person.

Here are some occasions when a thank-you note is particularly appropriate:

- As a follow-up to an introductory business meeting

- As a follow-up to a job interview

- After a business meal

- To show appreciation for support from staff members or colleagues

Writing a thank-you note doesn't have to be a major project. In fact, the most appreciated and memorable notes are those that are simple and sincere. Follow these three general guidelines for writing sincere and thoughtful thank-you notes:

1. **Handwrite them.** Handwriting gives your notes a personal touch. However, this guideline applies only if your handwriting is legible. If it isn't, stick to typing.

2. **Keep them short.** Three to four sentences is usually enough. Don't overdue the gratitude. Gushing makes most people feel uncomfortable and can sound fake.

3. **Be specific when possible.** "Thank you for your help writing the report last week" is much warmer and more personal than simply "Thank you for your help."

The following is an example of an effective thank-you note:

> Dear Diane,
>
> Thank you for taking the time to meet with me. The ideas generated by the committee will be useful in designing the program.
>
> Please convey my thanks to the other committee members. I look forward to working with all of you.
>
> Sincerely,
>
> Barbara

Exercise 11

WRITING TO COMMUNICATE

Using the skills you have learned in this section, rewrite the following business letter in the style of the Promotable Person.

Gentlemen:

Enclosed please find herewith the newly revised copy of the suggested proposal for your perusal. The proposal details our mutual understanding in regard to the installation of new piping for your building. We need for you to review it completely and give it a thorough approval.

Thanking you in advance for your time commitment to this project. Please return the signed copy as soon as possible.

Respectfully,

_____

_____

_____

_____

_____

_____

_____

_____

_____

_____

Now compare your rewritten version to this one:

> Dear Mr. Smith:
>
> I have enclosed the revised copy of our proposal detailing the installation of new piping in your building. Please review and make any changes needed.
>
> I look forward to working with you and will call you next week to discuss the proposal further.
>
> Sincerely,

Your rewrite should have stated the main points clearly and eliminated jargon, clichés, and unnecessary words.

STRENGTHENING YOUR SPEAKING SKILLS

Does the prospect of speaking in front of a group of people make you feel nervous? afraid? downright paralyzed? Well, rest assured, you're not alone. Fear of public speaking is one of the most common phobias plaguing business people today.

And yet, we are always speaking, whether it is at a meeting with a boss, with a customer, or in front of a group. All of these are perfect opportunities for visibility. It is therefore critical to develop the skills and confidence to speak effectively, no matter what the occasion or the audience. The Promotable Person is always ready to step into the spotlight.

While a few "butterflies in the stomach" are perfectly normal, the prospect of delivering an oral presentation should not—and need not—inspire fear. Nor should a lack of confidence in your speaking skills hold you back from reaching the next rung of the corporate ladder.

Public speaking actually breaks down into two key components: the substance of the presentation and the delivery. Both are equally important. And both can be successfully managed with a little time and preparation.

Creating a Road Map

An effective speaker is a lot like a good tour guide. As the speaker, you know the landscape and all the points of interest. It's your job to make the journey memorable for your audience.

Like a tour guide, you must plan the destination in advance and the route you will take to get there. In effect, you are creating a road map. And because the road map is the key to the success of your journey, you must devote as much time and attention as you can to creating it.

Keep these six important points in mind while preparing your road map:

1. **Know your PAL.**

   • **Purpose:** What do you want to say? What is the conclusion you want your audience to reach?

   • **Audience:** Who will be listening? What are their needs, their interests, their values? What will they gain by listening to what you have to say?

   • **Logistics:** Where will you be speaking and under what conditions? How large is the room? Will you be standing behind a lectern, or will you be able to move around? If you need a microphone, will one be available? Will you be using visual aids? How much time will you have? Are you part of a group? What time of day are you speaking?

2. **Start with the end in mind.** Never lose sight of your final destination. It's easy to wander off the main road and go off on tangents that lead to nowhere. You can't risk losing any member of your audience before you get to the end of your journey.

3. **Start strong.** Shock them. Excite them. Intrigue them. Just make sure you capture your audience's interest quickly. Remember, if you don't have your audience's attention at the beginning of your presentation, it's highly unlikely that you'll have it at the end.

4. **Don't make your audience sift through a "data dump."** One of the quickest ways to lose your audience is to recite page after page of dry facts and figures. Even if the information is of the utmost importance, you'll diminish its importance if you dump it on your audience in a great, tangled heap.

5. Use humor, stories, examples, and visual aids to illustrate and anchor your point. All of these add interest to your presentation. Even more important, people find it easier to understand and remember things they can visualize.

6. End strong and with conviction. Your audience has remained right in step with you throughout the journey. Now the final destination is in sight. This is the time to emphasize the key points you want them to remember and to urge them to go out and take appropriate action, or to reiterate the action you plan to take.

Writing the Speech

Now your road map is complete. The next step is to put your well-organized thoughts into words; that is, to write the speech or presentation. Every effective speech consists of three parts: the introduction, the body, and the conclusion

1. Introduction. Start with a "grabber" statement. This can be a story, a quote, a question, or something as simple as "At our last meeting, you asked me to...." The idea is to get the audience's attention quickly.

Be sure to let your audience know what's in it for them. Why should your audience pay attention to what you have to say? Why should they care? How will what you say affect them?

Establish your credibility. Let your audience know your background, experience, and expertise so they can view you as an authority on the subject. If your audience knows you already, you may not need to do this.

Preview what you're going to talk about. In other words, tell them what you're going to tell them. Keep it brief; you'll have plenty of opportunity to elaborate later.

2. Body. Keep the heart of your speech to three to five ideas. That's all an audience can absorb at one time. Make each idea count. One way to do this is to organize your ideas logically. Your audience won't be able to follow you if you randomly jump from one thought to another.

Use clear, simple language. If your audience is busy trying to define the terms or jargon you're using, they can't concentrate on the message you're trying to get across.

3. **Conclusion.** Tell them what you've already told them. In other words, restate your main points. You previewed your key ideas in the introduction, you elaborated on them in the body, and now you must summarize them.

Doing this will reinforce to audience members the action you want them to take or what action you plan to take. Don't beat it to death—keep it brief and to the point.

It Has to Sound As Good As It Looks

Congratulations! You've just written a great speech. It's packed with pertinent information. It's organized, powerful, and compelling. Now you're ready to go out there and knock 'em dead, right?

That's what Miriam, a talented research scientist, thought when her company asked her to present a paper at a conference. Knowing that it was important to her company and to her own professional future to deliver a well-organized presentation, she spent time mapping out and writing her speech. In fact, she was so confident in the strength and value of the research she would be presenting that she didn't feel the need to practice her delivery.

Unfortunately, when it came time to deliver the presentation at the conference, Miriam froze. Eventually, she was able to stumble her way through the presentation; however, she was so upset that she left before the question session ended.

Miriam was never asked to present again. And instead of continuing to rise through the ranks of her company, this promising scientist remains in the same research position, with no upward mobility in sight.

Overcoming Stage Fright

What happened to Miriam could happen to anyone. It's called *stage fright.* Even the most seasoned performers—actors, singers, dancers, and yes, public speakers—have been known to experience this feeling of irrational terror from time to time. But, in most cases, the show goes on because they know how to overcome it and use it to their advantage.

The best time to stop an attack of stage fright is before it begins. Because you can never predict when it's going to strike, you should take these three preventive steps every time you're scheduled to give a presentation:

- *Plan* what you have to say.

- *Prepare* the text of your presentation or, at the very least, prepare an outline.

- *Practice* giving your presentation out loud three to five times.

Miriam, the research scientist, knew she needed to plan and prepare her presentation. What she didn't realize was that content alone could not carry her. By neglecting to practice her presentation, she didn't give herself a chance to develop a comfortable delivery style. She didn't allow herself to become familiar with the flow and rhythm of her words and the sound of her own voice saying them. As a result, she was a prime candidate for a case of mind-blanking stage fright.

In all fairness, even the best prepared, most well-rehearsed speakers can be struck with stage fright. If, despite your best efforts, stage fright should strike you, here are a few tricks to help you channel those nerves into positive energy:

- *Breathe.* Many people actually forget to breathe when they're anxious or frightened. Focus on your breathing. Inhaling deeply and exhaling slowly can help you relax and regain your composure. Deep breathing also draws more oxygen into your body, making you feel fresher and more alert.

- *Visualize success.* Don't think about the things that might go wrong or worry that the audience might not like you. Create a mental image of yourself speaking with power and confidence. Imagine the audience on its feet applauding you.

- *Give yourself a pep talk.* Repeat to yourself: "I know my material. I am comfortable with my delivery. I am an effective speaker."

Handling Questions

They're awake. They're applauding. It's over, and you've done an admirable job. But wait—is that a raised hand? Someone wants to ask a *what?*

If you're going to give a presentation, you better be prepared to answer the questions your audience will almost certainly want to ask. The most important thing is to stay relaxed and have confidence in your knowledge of the material. You'll do just fine, especially if you keep these simple guidelines in mind:

- *Try to anticipate questions and practice responses to them.* Although you can't possibly anticipate every question your audience might come up with, you can have a good idea of what some of them are likely to be. Try to formulate responses to as many questions as you can prior to your presentation.

- *Maintain control.* Don't allow a question to make you angry or send you rambling off on a tangent. Don't allow one questioner to monopolize you. When someone asks a question, paraphrase what he or she has asked, answer the question, and then move on to the next person. If you announce time parameters for your question-and-answer period ("I have about five minutes to take questions"), you let the audience know you won't be opening a lengthy discussion.

- *Keep your answers brief and of general interest to the group.* If the questioner insists on asking you something that pertains specifically to himself or herself, arrange for a brief meeting at a later time. It's impolite to strike up a private conversation when you should be addressing the entire group.

PROMOTABLE ASSIGNMENTS

1. Make it a habit to check every document you write against the effective writing guidelines included in this chapter. After a few weeks, you'll find yourself doing it automatically.

2. Prepare a five-minute presentation about your job. Practice and tape record your presentation. Assess your strengths, and work on any areas you consider weak.

3. Look for places to present your ideas. Volunteer to speak at business meetings or at community organizations.

▲ *CHAPTER 7*

One-on-One Communication

Although writing and public speaking are important aspects of communication, the Promotable Person is also a master of one-on-one communication.

This chapter will focus on interpersonal, two-way communication. This statement may sound odd since *all* communication is two-way: someone sending a message and someone else receiving it. But the message that's sent isn't always the one received. And that's because many people simply don't know how to listen or to effectively say what they mean.

THE IMPORTANCE OF LISTENING

Studies show that we spend over 80 percent of our waking time communicating. Of that, we spend 45 percent listening. That might sound as if we spend a lot of time doing nothing. However, listening is a very important activity for these four major reasons:

1. **You gain information.** Clients, customers, and co-workers are constantly trying to tell you what they need. Listening allows you to understand and respond to those needs.

2. **You receive direction.** You've been taught since childhood to listen to directions. Some directions can help you do your job better, to accomplish daily tasks more easily. Some instructions can even be life-saving.

3. **You understand and connect with people better.** Active listening allows you to get a sense of the speaker's underlying feelings and, in turn, a good indication of what motivates him or her.

4. **It's the polite thing to do!** And that's reason enough for the Promotable Person.

If listening is so important and we do so much of it, then it must come naturally, right? Not really. Just because you have two functioning ears doesn't mean you know how to listen. Although you can probably recall personal experiences or incidents when listening proved particularly beneficial for you, you can probably also relate the negative consequences you've experienced due to poor listening.

Many people confuse *hearing* with *listening*. Actually, hearing is passive. You can't help but hear the sounds around you. In fact, if you don't want to hear certain sounds, you have to take active measures to block them out (e.g., put your hands over your ears or wear earplugs).

Listening is *not* passive. It requires real effort, not of the body, but of the mind. It requires concentration. Sounds easy enough. Until you try to do it. Sometimes trying to concentrate can require more effort—and seem more difficult—than actual physical labor. Fortunately, there are specific steps you can take to improve your ability to concentrate.

Here are five of them:

1. **Overcome distractions.** Not just external distractions, but internal ones as well. Find a quiet place for conversations, if possible. Hold all calls and visitors during meetings. And don't try to concentrate on an empty stomach—hunger is one of the most powerful distractions of all!

2. **Pay attention to body language—yours and the speaker's.** Establish and maintain eye contact, but don't stare. Don't cross your arms. It makes you look defensive and creates a barrier between you and the other person. Avoid distracting mannerisms such as pencil- or foot-tapping, hair-twirling, and fidgeting. When appropriate, mirror the speaker's body language and voice tempo to indicate that you're in harmony with him or her.

3. **Stop talking.** It's almost impossible to talk and listen at the same time. When you're listening for information, take notes, if it's appropriate. Remember the old Chinese proverb, "The palest ink is better than the best memory."

4. **Ask clarifying questions.** If you're not sure whether you've grasped the message the speaker was trying to convey or if you want more information, don't be afraid to ask questions. Speaking up is much better—and safer—than assuming. Some easy questions and statements you can use to encourage your speaker to elaborate are: "What else?", "What do you think about...?", "Tell me more about...", "Why do you think that...?"

5. **Paraphrase.** Quite simply, paraphrasing involves putting what the speaker has just said into your own words and repeating it. Paraphrasing serves two purposes. First, it ensures you that you've correctly understood what the speaker was trying to communicate. Second, it assures the speaker that you're really listening. Here's one example of paraphrasing:

   Speaker: "My babysitter was late, my car stalled, and my secretary called in sick."

   Listener: "It sounds as if this has been a difficult morning for you."

   Other examples of paraphrasing may begin with these phrases: "What you're saying is...", "Let me see if I understand...", or "Are you saying that...?"

ASSERTIVE COMMUNICATION

Just as listening is an important part of communication, so is being assertive.

What *is* assertive communication?

It isn't passive. Passive people consider only the needs of other people, never their own. Passive people are rarely promoted.

It isn't aggressive. Aggressive people consider only their own needs, even if they conflict with the needs of others. Unfortunately, some aggressive people do get promoted.

Assertive communication involves acknowledging how *you* think and feel while taking into account how *other* people think and feel. This balance provides the basis for a "win-win" form of communication, which is the most powerful communication of all.

Here are some tips for strengthening your assertive communications skills:

1. **Use "I" statements instead of "you" statements.** Say the following statements aloud and note the difference in the sound and effect of each:

   Statement 1: "I don't understand. Could you repeat that?"

   Statement 2: "You're not explaining it right. Say it again."

   The first statement is assertive. It doesn't accuse or blame the speaker. It shares responsibility.

   The second statement is aggressive. It accuses the speaker of being a poor communicator. It makes the speaker responsible for the receiver's failure to understand.

   Monitor yourself. Most people don't realize how frequently they use "you" statements.

2. **Keep statements short.** Say what you have to say and stop talking. If you continue talking, you're likely to talk yourself out of your position. Aimless rambling also tends to distract your listener and weaken your initial statement.

3. Use positive language. If it's not possible to use positive words, then at least keep your language neutral. Negative language makes people defensive and often makes them feel obligated to offer an excuse or rebuttal.

Read the following statements and notice the difference:

Negative: "You failed to return my phone call."

Neutral: "My phone call was not returned."

Positive: "Please return my phone calls in a timely manner."

4. Pay attention to your tone of voice. If your voice is too soft, you may be perceived as passive. If it's too loud, you may be perceived as aggressive. Maintain an even tone of voice that's somewhere in the middle—powerful and authoritative, yet not overwhelming and threatening.

5. Establish and maintain eye contact. Look people in the eye, but don't stare.

6. Watch your gestures. A pointed finger, crossed arms, or a pounding fist can convey aggression. Closed, tight, or nervous gestures such as playing with your fingers can be perceived as passive.

GIVING AND RECEIVING FEEDBACK

Sometimes communication involves telling others they've done something wrong or pointing out areas where they could improve. That kind of feedback is commonly known as criticism.

However, criticism doesn't have to be negative and hurtful. On the contrary, it can be quite helpful, depending on the spirit and manner in which it is delivered—and received.

Here are some ways to get your point across with sensitivity and tact:

1. Choose an appropriate place. Even when it's offered in a positive manner, criticism can be embarrassing. Don't make it worse by delivering your feedback in a public place such as in the middle of a hallway or at the coffee machine. Choose a private place where you aren't likely to be overheard.

2. **Choose an appropriate time.** When it comes to delivering criticism (and accepting it), some times are better than others. Don't pick a time when you—or the person to whom you're speaking—are preoccupied with a million other things. Wait until you can both sit down calmly and go over your feedback point by point.

3. **Describe the behavior; don't label the person.** "How could you be so stupid?" isn't constructive criticism. It offers nothing of value and succeeds only in making the listener defensive and in tearing down his or her self-esteem. Be specific. Help the listener understand exactly what behavior is unacceptable and why: "I am unhappy about the quality of your report" or "The data was not up to date."

4. **Describe the behavior you expect.** It's easier for people to meet your expectations if they know what they are. The listener should also come away with a clear understanding of why the recommended change in behavior is important—to you, to the company and, most of all, to his or her future as a Promotable Person.

   For example, if the data in a report is not up to date and the deadline was missed, you might say: "In the future, I expect you to do a computer search so the information is current. And remember, you must meet the deadline to show that you can handle assignments in a timely and professional manner before you can move up in this organization."

5. **Follow up in writing, if appropriate.** Some companies require this. Even if yours doesn't, it's a good idea in many situations, especially when you're a supervisor. Following up in writing accomplishes the following:

   • Reemphasizes key points and recommendations

   • Ensures that the listener clearly understands these points and recommendations

   • Underscores the importance of changing unacceptable behaviors

   • Provides a record of the interaction in case you need it later

There's only one thing more difficult than giving criticism. That's taking it. Yes, Promotable Person, sometimes you will be on the receiving end of criticism. It's a part of life in the corporate world. It's also part of the growth process, both professional and personal.

That's why as a Promotable Person, one of the most important skills you can develop is the ability to accept criticism as gracefully as you accept praise (or, at least, almost as gracefully). Perhaps even more important, you must be able to put criticism in perspective.

Okay, so you've been called into your boss's office. As soon as you sit down, the boss launches into a criticism of your work. You can react by giving your resignation right on the spot, or you can behave like the Promotable Person you are and take the following actions:

1. **Relax, breathe deeply, and remain calm.** Don't start fidgeting or exhibiting other nervous mannerisms. Above all, don't panic. You'll get through this.

2. **Don't get defensive.** At the first sign of a discouraging word, don't jump in with an excuse or rebuttal. Let the speaker finish. Listen to what he or she is saying.

3. **Consider the source.** Does the speaker have the knowledge, experience, or expertise to offer criticism? If the speaker isn't your boss, is it a person who has authority within the organization? Does the speaker have an ax to grind or an ulterior motive that could be the real basis for the criticism?

4. **Get specific examples.** The statement "You did a poor job" tells you only that the speaker is disappointed in your performance. You need to know why. If the criticism seems to be general or vague, don't hesitate to ask for specific examples. For instance, ask "What exactly were you unhappy with about the job?"

5. **Evaluate the validity of the criticism.** Nobody's perfect. You *will* make mistakes. And, even when you've done your best, there will be times when you can still improve.

6. **Accept constructive feedback and put it to use.** Take a little time to reflect on the speaker's points. Don't let your pride blind you to the value of constructive feedback, even if it's presented in the form of criticism. If that criticism is valid, acknowledge your mistake. Say: "You're right. The information wasn't up to date. It won't happen again." Put that feedback to good use. Use it to enhance your position as a professional and as a Promotable Person.

7. **Don't beat yourself up.** Don't dwell on it, don't lose sleep over it, and don't get paranoid. Yes, being criticized may embarrass you. Maybe even make you angry. But when it's over, it's over. Let it go. It's not worth getting ulcers over.

HANDLING THE DIFFICULT PERSON

In a perfect world, everyone would know how to communicate in a positive and assertive manner. There would be no angry confrontations. No antagonistic retorts. No hostile behavior. But this is the real world. Not everyone will have finely honed assertive communication skills.

Therefore, Promotable Person, it is up to you to maintain your composure and your professionalism at all times—even when others lose theirs. The following techniques will help you handle "difficult" people.

1. **Remember to keep using "I" statements.** Slipping into accusatory language can only fan the flames of the other person's anger and lead to increased hostility on both sides.

2. **Be a broken record.** Keep repeating your point over and over in an even tone of voice. Don't allow yourself to get sidetracked or provoked into an argument.

3. **Ask questions to clarify.** No matter what the person says, don't lash out. You can often stop a verbal attack cold by asking the speaker to clarify his or her statements. Some examples of questions you might ask would be: "Are you saying...?", "Why did you say that...?", "Would you explain why you think that...?"

Being a good listener and an assertive communicator are invaluable skills for everyone. To the Promotable Person, they are absolutely essential. Both take practice, but they can be learned. In time, they'll even become second nature.

PROMOTABLE ASSIGNMENTS

1. Keep an assertiveness diary. After a difficult discussion, record your thoughts and feelings, the circumstances, and the words you used. Watch for patterns. Where do you need to improve? If possible, ask a trusted colleague or family member to role play some of the common communication situations you have difficulty handling. Or write responses you might use the next time a particular difficult situation arises.

2. Pretend that you have to report back on a conversation. Practice your listening skills. Write the report.

▲ CHAPTER 8

Networking

*N*etworking is one of the most widely used buzzwords of this decade. In the movies and on television, a typical networking situation is often portrayed as a roomful of caricature "yuppie"-types sipping cocktails as they flit from person to person throwing kisses to the air and saying "Let's do lunch." The networkers are usually portrayed as shallow individuals who never really pay attention to whom they're talking to at the moment because they're all too busy looking around the room trying to spot someone who might be an even better contact.

In reality, networking is an excellent—and totally legitimate way—to initiate and cultivate important contacts, help you get the job you want, sell more products, or position yourself or your company to your best advantage. Although the old saying "It's not what you know, it's who you know" isn't totally accurate, networking can open many doors, including some that you may not even know existed.

Networking makes it possible for you to meet new and interesting people. Just as important, it gives new and interesting people the chance to meet you—and to discover for themselves what a Promotable Person you are.

One of the most recognizable and effective examples of networking can be seen in the broadcast media. Groups of radio and television stations across the country are organized into networks that relay programs broadcasting the same information and entertainment programs. As a member of the network, each station benefits from the collective purchasing power and production capabilities of the group rather than relying on its own funds to develop and produce its own programs.

Networking works best when it's viewed as a two-way street. Just as you would expect assistance and support from others in your network, they should be able to expect—and get—the same from you.

So, unlike what you might see in the movies and on television, real networking isn't a bunch of shallow people trying desperately to be "discovered" and catapulted to the top of the corporate ladder. The most effective networks consist of individuals who are genuinely interested in one another as colleagues and human beings.

SIX STEPS TO EFFECTIVE NETWORKING

Okay, so you understand the benefits of networking. You really want to get out there and do it. The problem is, you don't quite know where to begin.

Don't worry. Networking opportunities pop up every day, everywhere you go. The trick is to learn to recognize and take advantage of them. Fortunately, successful networking is a process that can be learned. Are you concerned that you don't have the personality for effective networking? Don't be. You can personalize your networking situations to suit your individual style and personality. To be successful at networking, it's important that you feel comfortable. So be yourself.

Keeping all of this in mind, it's time for you to start developing your own network. Here are six simple steps to get you started:

1. **Who do you already know?** The simplest way to begin networking is to make a list of people you already know. However, instead of alphabetizing your list as you would in a telephone book, organize the people you know into categories. Examples of some of these categories would be your friends, co-workers, neighbors, social or sports club members, doctor, dentist, banker, accountant, religious leader, customers, competitors, relatives, and so on.

   One of the best ways to do this is to make up a "network tree." Use the model on page 93 to get started. Chances are, once you've finished filling in the branches of your tree, you'll be pleasantly surprised at the number of people you know.

2. **Determine your objective.** If your objective is to increase your visibility in order to enhance your opportunities for promotion, you must focus on expanding the number and types of people you know within your organization and profession. However, keep in mind that every organization, profession, and community is different and that each offers unique networking opportunities. Keep an open mind and a sharp eye so you'll be sure to take full advantage of the opportunities available to you.

If your objective is to change jobs, you'll probably want to contact friends, relatives, professional associates, people you have worked with before, and even social contacts. Tell them what your goals are, why you want to leave your current job, and how you plan to market yourself.

Perhaps your objective is simply to meet and get to know other people for the sheer pleasure of it. Networking can really be fun, especially when you allow yourself to relax and enjoy it. As a Promotable Person, you also realize that the people you add to your "network tree" today could turn out to be your most valuable resources in the future.

Set small goals at first. For example, set out to meet one or two new people each week or month. Review your goals frequently, and as you reach them, cross them off your list. Be sure to reward yourself. Then set some new goals!

3. **Make the contact.** You can call, write, or simply approach the person. How you initiate the contact can depend on several different factors, including the circumstances, your relationship with the individual, and what feels most comfortable to you.

Plan ahead, keeping your objective in mind. What do you want your contact to know about you? What do you know about your contact? How can you help each other?

If you are initiating contact as a follow-up to a referral, be sure to mention the name of the person who referred you.

If you are planning to attend a business or social event, have your most impressive handshake and self-introduction ready. A self-introduction is your own personal ten-second commercial designed to tell people—in a clear, concise, and upbeat fashion—who you are and what you do. Here's an example:

> "Hello. I'm Sally Smith, an environmental engineer at ABC Corporation. I help our company comply with government regulations."

Exercise 12

MY NETWORK TREE

On each branch of your tree, fill in the names of the people you know.

Professional   Social

_____   _____
_____   _____
_____   _____
_____   _____

                                         Within your organization

Community   _____
_____   _____
_____   _____
_____   _____
_____

                                         Outside your organization
                                         _____

Others (church, children,   _____
sports, hobbies)   _____
_____   _____
_____
_____   Family
_____
_____   _____
                        M   _____
                        E   _____
                                         _____
                                         _____

4. Take advantage of every opportunity. View every person you come in contact with as a potential member of your network. Don't miss obvious opportunities to initiate contact. If, for example, you're by yourself at an association luncheon, look for someone who is standing alone. Go up to that person and introduce yourself. Look the person right in the eye and smile. Shake his or her hand. Asking a question such as "Have you been to an association function before?" is an easy way to start. Most people will be happy—and, in fact, relieved—that you have approached them. Once you ask a question, they will continue talking to you. Now you have made a new contact. Exchange business cards and note on the card how and where you met this new person. Because you never know when a new contact will become someone important in your life, be sure to follow up with a simple note or perhaps some information that would be of interest to this new person.

5. If it's not working, cut it short. Sometimes when you meet someone, it quickly becomes clear that the person isn't someone you would want to know better. Perhaps you find that you have absolutely nothing in common. There's no law that says you have to hit it off with every person you meet. However, the law of common courtesy does require you to be polite. Simply say, "It was nice talking to you. Please excuse me." Don't forget to smile and say good-bye.

6. Keep in contact with your network. Constantly enlarging your Rolodex or database is not enough. Now that you've made these new contacts, you must cultivate them. Here are a few simple suggestions for doing so:

- Send relevant articles.

- Acknowledge awards, promotions, or positive publicity your contact has received.

- Call to say hello.

- Schedule lunch.

- Look for ways to help others.

- Send thank-you notes when appropriate.

AVENUES FOR NETWORKING

After moving to a new city, Sandra joined two professional organizations. At a lunch meeting, she introduced herself to the person sitting next to her. After lunch, the woman said: "You have to meet my boss. We're looking for someone with your expertise." Sandra got the interview, and she was hired!

There are many ways that you, the Promotable Person, can increase your visibility. Here are just a few:

1. **Get out of your office.** Attend business and social functions. Join colleagues for lunch.

2. **Join company teams (golf, tennis, etc.).** Participate. You don't have to be a great player. Just get out there and have fun!

3. **Clip newspaper and magazine articles you think would be of interest to your contacts.** Send them along with a brief personal note or card.

4. **Be a volunteer.** In addition to meeting new people, volunteering gives you a chance to give something back to your community. Raise money for or give some of your time to a charity, work in a food kitchen or serve "meals-on-wheels," read at a senior citizens' center, coach a Little League team, or be a scorekeeper. Volunteer at the office, especially for cross-departmental activities. The results may be even more rewarding than you can imagine.

   Consider the following example: A supervisor from one of the training departments of a major regional bank that was restructuring volunteered to serve on the company's assessment team. When the restructuring was finished, this supervisor was promoted to manager of training. Why? As a member of the assessment team, he had worked closely with the new vice president of human resources.

5. **Make yourself visible.** Wherever you are, always be ready for new opportunities to meet and talk to people. Don't sit in a corner waiting to be approached. Make the first move.

   At meetings, for example, sit at the registration desk. Everyone has to stop there, so you'll get the chance to meet many people as well as renew acquaintances with others you've met before.

Serve on committees. And make sure you actively participate. This is a perfect opportunity to show your new contacts how creative and effective you can be.

Another way to create an impression and be noticed is to wear something noticeable—as long as it's in good taste. A smart-looking suit can help you make a very positive and lasting impression.

6. **Join organizations.** The most obvious are professional and trade associations. Another possibility is your local chamber of commerce.

Don't overlook the importance of participating in parent-teacher organizations and on volunteer committees. Or start your own group based on your professional or personal interests. First, check around to make sure a similar group doesn't already exist. Then, invite people you've met and would like to know better. Ask each person to invite a friend or a colleague.

7. **Move out of your comfort zone.** Look for unusual opportunities to network. Create new opportunities. For example, when you go on vacation in other cities or countries, attend association meetings that are being held at the time of your visit. Or contact local people who've been referred to you by friends and associates. You could also seek out groups that might be of interest to you, contact them, and ask if you may attend one of the meetings.

8. **Get published.** Submit articles to local newspapers or magazines, your company's newsletter, and association newsletters (yours and others). If none of these options work, self-publish and mail to your network.

9. **Offer to speak.** Look for speaking opportunities within your organization or professional association. And when you're attending meetings, don't just sit back, speak out!

10. **Specialize.** Become an expert on a particular topic (see Chapter 4) and people will seek you out.

Exercise 13

OPPORTUNITY CHECKLIST

Are you making the most of the opportunities available to you? Answer "yes" or "no" to the following questions to find out.

	Yes	No
1. Did you approach a "stranger" at your organization's last social event?	☐	☐
2. Do you say "hello" to people you don't know when you're waiting in line?	☐	☐
3. Do you keep your business cards with you at all times— even when you go on vacation?	☐	☐
4. Do you initiate follow-up with new people you've met?	☐	☐
5. Have you volunteered to speak at a meeting of your professional association?	☐	☐
6. When eating lunch in the cafeteria, have you joined people you didn't know? (Be sure to ask before you sit down; it's only polite.)	☐	☐
7. Do you belong to any professional organizations? If so, do you volunteer for committees?	☐	☐
8. Do you volunteer in your community? at work?	☐	☐
9. Have you submitted any suggestions for improvement within your organization? (To avoid stepping on anyone's toes, always follow your company's established suggestion procedures and systems.)	☐	☐
10. Do you send holiday cards to your contacts?	☐	☐

There are only two kinds of people in the world—those you already know and those you haven't met yet. Both of these groups provide countless opportunities for developing new friendships and valuable professional contacts. So get out there and start building your network now. As a Promotable Person, you'll be building the foundation for your future.

PROMOTABLE ASSIGNMENTS

1. Create your own ten-second commercial (your self-introduction). Try it out on a few friends and get their feedback. Did you speak clearly? Was your presentation understandable?

2. Introduce yourself to five new people within the next month. If appropriate, add them to your network.

PART 4

Making Impressions Count

▲ CHAPTER 9

Sending Appropriate Nonverbal Signals

In the movie *Working Woman,* the lead character dramatically transformed her professional image with a change of hairstyle, makeup, and wardrobe. Her understanding of the power of impressions is one of the things that made this "working woman" a Promotable Person.

Or consider the example of the man who wanted to move from his engineering position into management. After observing upper management, he changed from short-sleeved to long-sleeved shirts and shaved his unruly beard. It worked.

Standards of dress may vary throughout the country and within various industries, but one thing is constant no matter where you are or what business you're in: impressions count for the Promotable Person.

Just how are impressions made? For the most part, they are based on the signals you send to other people. Some of these signals are verbal. But the majority are not. In fact, many times, most people aren't even aware that they're sending signals.

Research shows that over 90 percent of face-to-face communication is nonverbal. In other words, the nonverbal signals you send speak volumes more than your words. Knowing this, the Promotable Person is careful to keep verbal and nonverbal messages consistent.

CREATING A PROFESSIONAL VISUAL IMAGE

The visual image you present is one of the most important means of nonverbal communication. Your visual image consists of six major components:

1. Body language

2. Eye contact

3. Facial expressions

4. Use of space

5. Wardrobe

6. Grooming

1. **Body language.** We do more than half of our communicating through posture and gestures—that is, through our *body language*. What is *your* body saying about you? The following lists of do's and don'ts should give you a pretty good idea.

Posture: Standing

Don't	*Do*
• Slouch	• Stand straight (feet 4"-8" apart)
• Shift feet	• Keep feet still
• Sway	• Keep shoulders relaxed

Posture: Seated

Don't	*Do*
• Slouch or sprawl	• Sit up straight
• Broaden thighs (women)	• Cross legs at ankles
• Cross legs in feminine manner (men)	• Lean slightly forward

Movement

Don't	*Do*
• Drag feet	• Move purposefully
• Clomp or shuffle	• Stride deliberately
• Bend from the waist	• Bend from the knees when picking up an object

Gestures

Don't	*Do*
• Put hands on hips	• Gesture with open palms
• Cross arms	• Use gestures to reinforce the message
• Fiddle with things in your pocket	• Vary your gestures
• Point your finger or pound your fist to reinforce points	

Facial Expressions

Don't	*Do*
• Frown	• Wear a pleasant expression and smile when appropriate
• Stare	• Make direct eye contact (see section on eye contact)
• Shift your eyes (see section on eye contact)	• Be animated

Distracting Behaviors

Don't

- Scratch or pick your nose
- Tug or play with your hair
- Comb your hair in public
- Drum your fingers
- Play with, pick, or bite your fingernails
- Tap your feet
- Put on makeup or nail polish in public
- Pick your teeth
- Fidget
- Straighten up paper/paper clips
- Click pens
- Chew gum
- Crowd people's space

2. **Eye contact.** Look people in the eye. It shows that you are at ease and interested in what they are saying. Don't let your eyes roam. It gives the impression that your attention is wandering. Even worse, it can make you look "shifty-eyed," like someone who has something to hide.

Be careful not to gaze so intensely and unwaveringly that you make people feel as if they're under minute scrutiny or that you're trying to stare them down. Be natural, be polite, and, for heaven's sake, remember to blink every once in a while.

3. Facial expressions. You wouldn't sit through a funeral with a big smile on your face. And you wouldn't frown if someone handed you a wonderful gift. Use the same common sense in your use of facial expressions in business.

Be animated, but not exaggerated. Your facial expressions should be appropriate to the circumstances and the conversation. Above all, look interested in what the other person is saying. The Promotable Person knows how to make others feel important without ever saying a word.

4. Use of space. The best rule to remember in business is to keep everyone at arm's length. That doesn't mean being cold and aloof. It means maintaining a comfortable physical distance between you and anyone to whom you are speaking. The most comfortable distance is literally "arm's length," about 36 inches.

People who stand too close to others can be intimidating. It can be viewed as a power play or assumption of intimacy. So always remember to respect the other person's "personal space." Keep your distance.

5. Wardrobe. If you want to play the game, you have to wear the uniform. Everybody knows that sports teams wear one. But did you realize that every corporate team has a uniform of its own as well?

There are no hard-and-fast rules for corporate dressing. The best guideline is to follow the example of upper management. (Make sure the upper management person you choose is a good role model.) That doesn't mean you have to look like a clone of your boss. It simply means that you could use him or her as a guide to developing your own personal style.

Even if the dress code in your organization tends to be casual, it's still important to keep your look polished, pulled together, and professional. The charts on pages 108-110 will give you an idea of the items you'll need for a complete professional wardrobe.

When selecting your business wardrobe, ask yourself these three questions:

1. Is it appropriate for my particular job, my position, my industry, and my organization?

2. Is the message I'm sending one of competence and professionalism?

3. Will it work for me? Remember, not everything suits every individual's style and taste. You can bend and even sometimes break the rules as long as you understand the consequences and think it through.

Finally, remember this: Always dress for the position you want to achieve. Looking professional is a plus no matter what position you currently hold.

Business Wardrobe Basics for Women

Clothing

- One black or gray suit
- One dark burgundy suit
- One navy suit
- One contrasting jacket and skirt
- One two-piece dress (in silk or 100 percent rayon)
- Several white/off-white blouses
- Five solid-color blouses
- Two pastel or print blouses

Accessories

- One scarf that picks up colors from your suit (always choose 100 percent silk because it knots and ties the best)
- One pair of black pumps (2" heels)
- One pair of navy or taupe pumps
- Six pairs of neutral or taupe hosiery
- One black leather bag
- Two leather belts, one navy and one black
- One all-weather coat
- One black, brown, or burgundy briefcase
- One pair each: gold, silver, good costume earrings

Suits should be wool or good quality blends. Avoid leather, suede, ultrasuede, corduroy, velvet, velour, denim, satin, and chiffon.

Go easy on the jewelry. Don't wear anything that jangles or makes noise. Wear the best watch you can afford.

Business Wardrobe Basics for Men

Clothing

- Solid-color navy suit
- Solid-color gray suit
- Pinstriped navy suit
- Pinstriped gray suit
- Charcoal-gray suit
- Navy sport coat, gray trousers
- Six white cotton shirts, long sleeve
- Blue or pinstriped shirt

Accessories

- Five pairs of black socks
- Two pairs of navy socks
- Four burgundy/red print or striped silk ties
- Two patterned silk ties
- Two navy/mauve ties
- One black leather belt
- Leather briefcase
- One pair black lace-up shoes
- One pair black or cordovan slip-on shoes

Suits should be wool blend because they resist wrinkling and can be worn all year round. For warmer climates or seasons, you might choose cotton pincord or poplin.

Be aware of the colors you choose. Each one sends a message of its own. For example, navy, gray, and charcoal are powerful colors (pinstripes add even more power). Black can be intimidating, while blue is usually perceived as friendly. Avoid brown—many people have a negative reaction to it.

Ties should be approximately 3 inches wide and 100 percent silk (no bow ties, please). Small geometric prints and stripes are good choices. So are paisleys with subdued patterns. Your tie and suit colors should complement each other, but not match.

Choose a quality watch in sterling silver, gold, or stainless steel.

Business Casual Guidelines: Dressing Down on Your Way Up

In an increasing number of businesses and circumstances, dress codes are relaxing. But be careful: Casual can have more than one connotation. Dress that may be considered perfectly acceptable for social occasions may not be at all appropriate for the office. Keep in mind, it's still business. So even on officially designated "dress-down days," it's still important to maintain a well-groomed, "business-ready" appearance.

Here are some guidelines to help you look the part of the Promotable Person, even when the dress code is strictly casual. (Depending on the industry or area of the country, these may vary, so use your best judgment.)

Men

Do's

- Khakis, chino pants
- Collared shirts
- Slip-on shoes
- Socks

Don'ts

- Shorts
- Jeans
- T-shirts
- Tank tops
- Sneakers or sandals

Women

Do's

- Skirts
- Blouses or collared shirts
- Skorts (shorts that look like skirts)
- Casual dresses
- Flats with stockings
- Slacks

Don'ts

- Shorts
- Jeans
- Stretch pants
- Sundresses
- Sleeveless tops or tank tops
- Sneakers or sandals

6. Grooming. Good grooming goes hand in hand with wardrobe in creating a professional appearance. You can wear the most expensive and well-tailored suit to a meeting with an important client and still make a lousy impression if your hair is too long for your particular field or the buttons on your sleeve are missing. The following lists contain some essential grooming guidelines. Although some guidelines may seem obvious, you'd be surprised at how often some "professionals" overlook them.

Women

- Lipstick blotted
- Hair out of face
- No distracting or noisy jewelry
- Limited makeup
- No facial hairs
- No low-cut or tight clothing
- Nothing too frilly or "girlish"
- Hide slip and bra straps
- Avoid designer labels that show
- Limited jewelry
- Hosiery without runs or snags

Men

- Well-knotted tie
- Pressed collar
- Neat hair length
- Trimmed facial hair
- No five o'clock shadow
- Nose hairs clipped
- Jackets that button
- Buttoned double-breasted jackets
- Mid-calf-length hose with good elastic
- Long-sleeve shirt with cuffs showing 3/5 to 5/8 of an inch below the jacket sleeve
- Trouser legs that break at front of shoe and taper down in the back

Both

- Clean hair (no dandruff)
- Clean, unspotted, lint-free, well-pressed clothing
- All buttons and hems sewn
- Eyeglasses: clear, well-fitted, no glasses hanging on chains
- Polished, straight, white teeth
- Clean breath
- Handkerchief in pocket or purse
- No strong perfume or cologne
- Clean and groomed nails
- Polished shoes

SENDING THE RIGHT SIGNALS: VOCAL

Your visual image is one means of nonverbal communication. But it isn't the only one. In fact, one of the most powerful nonverbal communication tools you have is your voice.

Why is the voice a *nonverbal* communication tool? Simple. The vocal signals you send can be very different from the words you say. In fact, depending on how you use your voice, you can make the same words mean many different things. For example, try saying the phrase "When I deal with companies your size." Say it once, making it sound as if it were a compliment. Now say it again, making it sound as if it were an insult.

To make it sound complimentary, emphasize the word *size*.

To make it sound insulting, emphasize the word *your*.

No big deal, right? Well, it was for the salesman who inadvertently chose the wrong way to say it. This simple phrase cost that man a one-million-dollar sale.

See how your voice can enhance—or undermine—your professional image and your promotability?

If you want to determine whether your voice is that of a Promotable Person, consider the following five factors:

1. **Pitch.** Some people's voices are naturally higher-pitched, some naturally lower. While research has shown that people tend to equate lower voices with higher levels of credibility, not everyone is expected to sound like a radio announcer. However, you can slowly lower the pitch of your voice using the following techniques:

   • Remember to breathe.

   • Practice raising and lowering your pitch by reading out loud for five minutes each day.

   • Drop your chin, just a little, for increased air flow.

2. Volume. A person with an excessively loud voice is likely to be regarded as overbearing. A person with an extremely soft voice is likely to be regarded as timid. A person who knows how to be heard without needing to shout is likely to be regarded as a Promotable Person.

You can assess the volume of your voice by tape recording your end of a conversation. Did your voice sound jarringly loud?

Or did you have to turn up the sound when you played back the tape? Either way, it isn't your tape player that needs the volume adjusted. It's your voice.

3. Rate. Unless you're an auctioneer, faster is not more impressive when it comes to speech. On the other hand, speak too slowly and you're likely to lose the attention of your audience long before you get to the point.

The average speaking rate has been calculated to be somewhere between 120 and 160 words a minute. Test yourself to see if your speaking rate falls between that range.

Of course, speaking rates vary in different parts of the country. But no matter where you are or where you're from, it's important to be aware and in control of the message your rate of speech is communicating about you.

People who speak too quickly are often perceived as nervous, rude, or untrustworthy. People who speak too slowly are often perceived as slow-witted, unintelligent, or indecisive. Hardly the traits that would be used to describe the Promotable Person.

Exercise 14

IMPRESSIONS QUOTIENT

Before you go to work tomorrow or as you prepare for your next big meeting or interview, measure your IQ (Impressions Quotient) by answering "yes" or "no" to the following questions:

	Yes	No
1. Is there anything in my appearance or grooming that is inappropriate?	☐	☐
2. Is my posture relaxed or too rigid?	☐	☐
3. Am I aware of my facial expressions when I am speaking or when others are speaking?	☐	☐
4. Do I avoid eye contact or stare at people when I am speaking or when they are speaking to me?	☐	☐
5. Do I overuse gestures when I speak?	☐	☐
6. Do I play with my hair or my tie, tap my feet, crack my knuckles, or play with change in my pocket?	☐	☐
7. Do I touch acquaintances when I speak to them?	☐	☐
8. Do I invade other people's space when I communicate?	☐	☐
9. Is my voice too soft, too loud, too fast, too slow, or just plain monotonous?	☐	☐
10. When speaking, do I fill in pauses with meaningless interjections (e.g., "um," "you know," "okay")?	☐	☐

If you find that your IQ could use some boosting, identify the specific behaviors you need to change—then go back through this chapter and note the behaviors that characterize the Promotable Person. Practice these appropriate behaviors every day, everywhere—at home as well as at work. Keep reinforcing these behaviors. Remember, if you look, act, and talk like the Promotable Person, you are the Promotable Person.

PROMOTABLE ASSIGNMENTS

1. Select an article from a magazine or newspaper. Read it aloud, timing yourself with a stopwatch. When you have finished, figure out your rate of speech, the number of words you say per minute. If your rate is not within the range of 120 to 160 words per minute, read the article again until you are within the range.

2. Read aloud into a tape recorder, exaggerating your diction so that you pronounce every syllable completely and clearly. Keep repeating this exercise until you no longer need to make a conscious effort to use proper diction.

▲ *CHAPTER 10*

Manners Matter

You've no doubt heard the old adage "nice guys finish last." Well, when it comes to competing in today's business world, nothing could be further from the truth.

The reality is that you—and your organization—are constantly being judged as much by your manners as by your technical capabilities. And "nice guys"—the individuals and organizations that consistently demonstrate courtesy and respect for others—are usually the ones that finish first in terms of business success.

Think of it this way: Would you rather do business with someone who treats you with courtesy and respect or someone who treats you in an off-handed or rude fashion? Whether you're dealing with a client, co-worker, or supervisor, good manners make a good impression. And a good impression is what makes you a Promotable Person.

Business etiquette is not rocket science. Most of the time, it is really just a matter of common sense. If you make it a rule to treat others as you would like to be treated yourself, you can't go wrong.

COMMON COURTESY

With etiquette, it's the little everyday niceties that make the biggest impression. These everyday niceties are called *common courtesies*. Here are twenty-five of the most important ones:

1. Say good morning and good night.

2. Say please and thank you when making a request.

3. Recognize the work of others.

4. Make sure everyone at a meeting or in a group knows one another; make introductions when necessary.

5. Take the initiative to introduce yourself.

6. Shake hands properly (firm, but not bone-crushing; two to three pumps).

7. Listen to others when they speak.

8. Put people at ease by starting conversations and making "small talk."

9. Dress appropriately.

10. Arrive on time and prepared for meetings.

11. Participate in meetings.

12. Answer the telephone graciously.

13. Show courtesy in the use of electronic communications devices (e.g., keep answering machine or voice mail messages brief and to the point, don't fax pages and pages of unsolicited materials, don't use machines to screen calls).

14. Conduct yourself honestly and ethically.

15. Acknowledge the help of others; give compliments.

16. Don't use foul language, tasteless humor, put-downs, or sarcasm.

17. Answer mail in a timely manner, including RSVPs.

18. Treat public property with respect (e.g., coffee machines, copiers, fax machines, office equipment, refrigerators).

19. Treat public space with respect (e.g., leave restrooms, meeting rooms, and cafeterias clean and in order).

20. Honor other people's "personal space" and right to privacy (e.g., knock on doors before entering, don't hover, don't touch things that don't belong to you, don't read over other people's shoulders, don't listen in on other people's conversations).

21. Don't speak loudly enough to disrupt others.

22. Don't spread gossip.

23. Don't discuss business in inappropriate places (e.g., in hallways, public places, at close tables in restaurants).

24. Don't cut people off in parking lots.

25. Don't park in spaces reserved for people with disabilities.

ETIQUETTE OUTSIDE THE OFFICE

Who says work isn't a picnic...or a day on the golf course...or a night at the opera? The Promotable Person knows that business isn't always conducted from behind a desk or around a conference table.

Social events and occasions provide important opportunities for you to get to know your bosses, co-workers, and clients—and for them to get to know you—on a different, more personal level. How you interact socially can have a tremendous negative or positive impact on your business relationships—and on your promotability.

The main thing to remember when fun is on the agenda is to maintain your company manners. No matter how informal, dressed down, or easy-going the atmosphere, it's still business. In other words, don't do or say anything that you wouldn't do or say in the office.

No matter what the occasion, even if it's a cocktail party, limit your consumption of alcohol. Even if you think you can "hold your liquor" without becoming sloppy, obnoxious, loose-tongued or sick, avoid excessive drinking. Other unattractive behaviors include gossiping, flirting, loudness, and telling off-color or offensive jokes or stories.

Treat everyone with respectful friendliness. Remember, too much familiarity can breed contempt, especially if you overstep boundaries that have been well established. For example, if you don't address your boss by first name in the office, don't do it at a party.

Be discrete about sharing the details of your personal life. Even though no one really has the right to pass judgment about anything you do on your own time, the fact is that many people do. And that judgment can make a big difference in how they view and treat you as a professional.

Dress appropriately for the occasion—and for your position as a Promotable Person. Casual may be the dress code for the company picnic, but that doesn't mean torn T-shirts, ratty jeans, short-short skirts, and plunging necklines.

Get out and mingle. Talk with those outside your familiar office "clique." Keep business talk to a minimum.

If the event is a family affair, make sure your family represents you well. To avoid an unintentional, but potentially deadly, slip of the tongue, brief your spouse or "significant other" on the political and personality particulars of your office. Don't let your children run wild.

Above all, try to look as if you're having fun. Even better, try to really have fun. Honestly, it's possible as long as you keep your perspective and remember to mind your manners.

The following sections offer a few additional guidelines to help you enhance your professional image in social settings.

Office Parties

- Attend. It's part of being a team player.

- Arrive on time. This is not the time to make a dramatic entrance.

- Use the opportunity to expand your network. Make the rounds and get to know supervisors and co-workers in other departments.

- If there is dancing, don't stick with one partner, unless it's your spouse. That's how office gossip starts. Women may certainly ask men to dance.

- Plan to stay an appropriate length of time. Don't be the first to leave and, for heaven's sake, don't be the last.

- Keep smiling, even if the party is dull.

- Even though your behavior will be exemplary, someone else is bound to do or say something at an office party that will prove to be embarrassing in the days to come. Be discrete. Even if the boss decides to dance with a lampshade on his head, never mention it again.

- Acknowledge the people who organized the party with a written thank you.

Cocktail Parties

- Always RSVP to the host or hostess by the specified date to allow time for planning and ordering appropriate amounts of food and drink.

- If you're unsure of the dress code (e.g., business attire, cocktail attire, etc.), ask the host or hostess.

- Eat a snack before you get to the party. Hovering over the hors d'oeuvres is bad form.

- Carry your drink in your left hand to keep your right hand free for handshakes.

- Don't smoke.

- Don't be the last to leave the party. An hour or two is usually an appropriate stay. Be sensitive to cues such as other guests beginning to leave, the host or hostess abandoning the bar, or offering coffee "for the road" to let you know the party's over.

- Follow up the party with a thank-you note to the host or hostess and spouse.

Company Picnic

- Volunteer to help with organization or clean-up. This will give you a good opportunity to become better acquainted with your co-workers.

- Participate in activities. So what if you haven't entered a three-legged race since you were eight. Smile, be a good sport, and give it all you've got. Who knows? You just might have fun.

At the Theater or Sporting Event

- If you are the host, you pay for the tickets.

- Prior to the event, familiarize yourself with what you're going to be seeing, whether it's a play, an opera, a ballet, or a football game. A little knowledge will enhance your enjoyment and enable you to make intelligent conversation.

- If you eat a heavy meal prior to attending the theater, you might find yourself snoring before the curtain rises. Eat lightly and avoid alcohol.

- At a sporting event, refrain from booing, hissing, shouting, and other unseemly behavior—even if your favorite team is losing.

Participating in a Sporting Event

- If the sport is new to you, learn the rules, practice, and if necessary, get coaching in advance.

- Be a good sport. Be on time, bring any required equipment, don't brag, don't throw temper tantrums, and don't complain.

- Be prepared to lose—or win—graciously.

Finally, there's the event of events—the stuff of sitcoms, movies, and nightmares—

Dinner at the Boss's House

- Arrive promptly. Late isn't fashionable when the roast is drying out in the oven.

- Bring a gift or send one ahead of time. Flowers or candies are usually safe choices.

- Don't initiate business conversation, and stay away from topics that might be controversial (e.g., politics, religion, the boss's son's job performance in your department, etc.). Include everyone in your conversation.

- Eat what is served, unless you have an allergy or other medical condition. If you must decline, do so graciously and quietly. Offer sincere compliments about the table setting, meal, and so forth.

- Don't rush off after the table is cleared. But don't stay around until your hosts feel obliged to offer pillows and blankets. Be sensitive to cues from your hosts or use your own judgment and initiate your exit after an appropriate period of after-dinner conversation.

- Send a thank-you note to the boss and his or her spouse.

INTERNATIONAL ETIQUETTE

As a Promotable Person in an increasingly global economic environment, you may well find yourself doing business with people from other countries and other cultures; therefore, it is important to remember that not all the common courtesies apply on a universal basis. Rules about eye contact, personal space, appropriate greetings, and so on often vary from culture to culture. What may be considered a courteous gesture in this country may be viewed as an insult in another.

The Promotable Person finds out the specific etiquette rules of the country or culture that he or she intends to do business with. If you know your business will be requiring travel abroad, take the time to do some reading and to prepare before you go. If representatives from companies overseas will be visiting you here, find out how you can make them feel most welcome and at home.

While the nuances of etiquette may not be universal, one thing is: good manners are good business. No matter where or with whom you do business, following etiquette guidelines will make others—as well as you—feel more comfortable interacting.

You will be more relaxed and better able to focus on the business at hand when you don't have to worry about whether or not something you do or say might be perceived as improper or offensive. Your overall confidence will increase and, with it, your effectiveness as a professional and your status as a Promotable Person.

▲ CHAPTER 11

Information Age Etiquette

Modern-day equipment and technology provide us with many time-saving conveniences in the workplace, but they have also opened up a whole new area where the Promotable Person must follow proper etiquette and protocol.

THE TELEPHONE

Have you ever wondered what your working day would be like without the telephone? Okay, so sometimes the thought of getting through an entire day without being interrupted by a million callers with questions, requests, or complaints may seem quite appealing. But the Promotable Person knows better than to view the telephone as a necessary nuisance. He or she recognizes its value and importance in a world where more and more business is being conducted via electronic media.

Like any powerful tool, the telephone can be effective only when it's used correctly. That means more than knowing how to program in your automatic dial numbers or where the "hold" button is located. It means knowing and observing telephone etiquette.

Actually, all telephone etiquette is based on two basic guidelines:

1. When you're the caller, always remember that the person you're calling is probably very busy and that yours may well be the fifth, sixth, or even tenth call he or she has received in the past hour.

2. When you're the person being called, always remember that as soon as you pick up the phone, the caller automatically becomes your number one priority. No matter what you're doing, no matter how busy or aggravated you may be, you should sound pleasant (it helps to smile before you say "hello"), professional, and ready to give the caller your full attention.

Of course, sometimes you just can't drop what you're doing to take a phone call. That's perfectly acceptable. What isn't acceptable is screening your calls with an answering machine or having your secretary (or co-worker) ask "Who's calling?" before acknowledging whether you're available or not. This kind of obvious call screening can convey an inflated sense of self-importance to all callers, and even worse, be insulting to callers who feel they've been "screened out."

Return all calls within twenty-four hours. If you're going on vacation or know that you won't be available for an extended period, make sure your secretary or any co-workers who may answer your phone relay that information to all callers. If you use an answering machine or voice mail, include that information in your message.

Anytime you tell someone you'll call at a specific time, consider it an appointment. The same applies if someone tells you he or she will call you at a specific time. If, for any reason, you won't be available at the predetermined time, be sure to call or have someone else call to reschedule. Let the person know when you will be available to talk. Then when you do finally connect, apologize for the inconvenience and thank the person for waiting.

Make Every Conversation Count

The way you answer the phone sets the tone for the entire conversation. The image your voice and manner project to the caller—particularly if that person is someone you've never met—may well determine whether he or she wants to do business with you.

Your greeting should immediately establish not only your identity but also your professionalism. If the call is from outside the company, identify your company too. For example "Good morning, Jones and Company, Sharon Stephens speaking." If the call originated from an internal source, identify yourself and, if you share the phone, your department. For example, "Hello, this is Sharon Stephens" or "Marketing Department, Sharon Stephens speaking."

Even if you're in an office full of people, keep your focus on the caller. Avoid side conversations with co-workers. They are distracting to you and annoying to the caller.

If you must transfer a call, give the caller the extension number of the person to whom the call is being transferred. That way, if you are accidentally disconnected, the caller won't have to go through the whole process again.

Would you ever take a client on a drive to the middle of nowhere and then just disappear for hours at a time? Of course not! But that's just how people feel when they're put on hold for long periods of time. If you must put someone on hold during the course of a conversation, ask first and wait for the person to give permission. Get back on the line as quickly as possible. Be sure to thank the person for holding. If you know the wait will be more than a few seconds, ask the person whether you can call back. Suspending someone on hold for long periods of time shows a blatant disrespect for that person's time. If you accidentally push a wrong button or become disconnected for some other reason, call the person back immediately.

Caller Courtesy

Before placing any business call, think about what you want to accomplish. Be organized. If necessary, write down the key points you want to cover. Have any reference files or other materials ready and easily accessible.

Immediately identify yourself to the person who answers the phone. For example, "Hello, this is John Madison of XYZ Corporation. Is Ms. Smith available?"

If the person you're calling is not available, always leave your number, even if it's someone you call on a regular basis. You can't assume that the person you're calling has your number memorized, and it's not polite or professional to make your contact search for your number to call you back.

Provide specific information on when you can be reached, especially if you are on the road or know you will be out of the office at a particular time. If you are calling long distance, offer to call back at a predetermined time. Don't assume the other party will want to bear the expense.

When you do reach your party, immediately explain the purpose and probable length of your call. Just launching into a lengthy conversation is a lot like dropping in on someone in the middle of a workday. You really don't know what you're interrupting or whether the person has time for your visit. If it isn't a good time, ask when would be a better time for you to call back.

It's a Good Time for Good-bye

When the conversation is over, don't drag it out or let it sputter to a clumsy close. Conclude with a positive, upbeat statement such as "I'll have that information to you by 10:00 Monday morning" or "It's been nice talking to you."

Make a note of any follow-up action you have to take—and then make sure you take it. If you promise to deliver information by 10:00 Monday morning, make sure it gets there. Some conversations, such as those involving verbal orders or agreements, should be confirmed in writing. Make sure you do it as soon as possible so it doesn't slip your mind.

ANSWERING MACHINES AND VOICE MAIL

Most people perceive answering machines and voice mail as necessary evils. Many feel uncomfortable talking to a machine in the first place, and even more uncomfortable if the message on the machine is abrupt or flippant.

Therefore, it's important to make your technological answering aids as "caller-friendly" as possible. The most important thing is to identify yourself by your full name so your caller knows that he or she has reached the right party. If possible, record the approximate time you expect to return or how frequently you call in to retrieve messages. Then give the caller instructions for leaving a message. For example, is there a time limit for messages? Does the machine automatically record the time and date of the call, or does the caller need to provide this information? Should the caller begin speaking at the tone or will there be several beeps followed by a long tone before recording will begin? Above all, make sure the machine is on and functioning before you go out.

When you leave a message on someone else's answering machine or voice mail, speak slowly and clearly. Begin by stating your name and phone number. Don't say anything that others shouldn't overhear. You never know who's standing next to an answering machine or who may access someone else's voice mail (even though that goes beyond impoliteness). Keep your message as brief as possible. No one wants to listen to a long recitation, especially if the person is retrieving messages from the road. Repeat your name and phone number at the end of the message. If necessary, exit the system before hanging up.

SPEAKER PHONES AND TELECONFERENCING

Speaker phones may be a great convenience to you, but not many people want everything they say to be broadcast to the immediate world. To avoid embarrassing situations—or revelations—ask permission before putting anyone on a speaker phone. Also be sure to identify other people who are in the room or who may be within hearing distance.

Teleconferencing is one of the technological wonders of modern business life, bringing together people all over town, the country, and even the globe with the press of just a few buttons. As with any gathering, every teleconferencing situation needs a "host" to introduce the various parties and to keep the flow of conversation moving forward. The host should begin the meeting by identifying all the participating parties by name. It is also his or her job to address the parties by name as they speak and, if necessary, to invite more reticent participants to share their views.

CAR PHONES

There's no doubt about it—car phones have been a boon for today's businessperson, especially those who spend a lot of time on the road. If you're tied up in traffic, you can call to say you'll be late. If you need some information in a hurry, you can get it no matter where you are. A car phone can even be a life-saver in emergency situations.

However, driving while talking on the phone can be dangerous—both to you and to all the other drivers on the road. No matter how bright, professional, and capable you may be, it's impossible to give your full attention to two things at the same time. Either your driving will distract you from your conversation or, worse yet, your conversation will distract you from your driving.

Use your car phone only when necessary. If possible, pull out of traffic or wait until you are stopped or parked.

Tell the party you're calling that you're on a car phone. That way, if you fade in and out or get cut off, the other person will know why.

Try to reduce distracting or distorting background noise by turning off your radio, rolling up your windows, turning down your air conditioning, and so on.

If you want to call others on their car phones, ask permission first. Incoming calls are charged to the car phone owner.

FAX MACHINES

Remember how much people used to complain about junk mail? Well, thanks to modern technology, many of us now find ourselves inundated by yet another form of unsolicited correspondence—the junk fax.

When used properly, facsimile machines can be a tremendous time saver, sending words and images anywhere in the world within seconds. However, in most offices, unsolicited faxes are considered, at best, a waste of paper and, quite often, a major nuisance. Some companies only release their fax numbers on a "need-to-know" basis in an attempt to reduce the volume of unsolicited transmissions.

Send faxes only when they're requested or expected. If you plan to transmit several pages, call ahead to get permission and ensure that you're not tying up the other person's fax machine at a peak time of day. If possible, send faxes at times when your machine—and the recipient's machine—are least likely to be in use. Early morning or lunchtime are usually slow faxing times.

Be sure your cover sheet includes all pertinent information, such as the recipient's name and department, your name and phone number, the number of pages in the transmission, the time and date sent, and any message. Indicate clearly whether delivery is urgent or time-sensitive.

If you share a fax machine and find a transmission that has come in, put it in the recipient's mail box. Don't read past the cover page. (As a sender, you can't assume that everyone will follow these guidelines. To be safe, don't send any information or include any comments over a fax machine that may be confidential or inappropriate for others to read.) Never reprogram a shared fax without permission. That includes deleting or otherwise changing automatic dial numbers. After using the machine, refill the paper if necessary. If there is a paper jam, fix it. If service or repairs are needed, notify the appropriate person. Don't automatically assume others will clean up after you.

131

OTHER TECHNOLOGICAL ADVANCES

TDD services (telecommunications devices for the deaf) enable the hearing impaired to communicate via telephone. When communicating with someone via a TDD service, speak a little more slowly than usual and say "go ahead" when you're ready for a reply. Otherwise, communicating with these devices is very much like speaking directly to the person you're calling.

Beepers—you hear their distinctive high-pitched tones at meetings, at restaurants, at the ballpark, just about everywhere. If yours goes off in a meeting or other inopportune place, turn it off immediately, excuse yourself, and leave the room to make your call.

PROMOTABLE EXERCISE

When you record a voice-mail message, get into the habit of playing it back before hanging up, if possible. Pay attention to your voice. Record the message over again if you're not satisfied with the way you sound. You are making an impression—good or bad—with every voice message you leave.

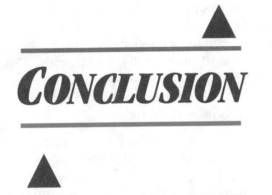

CONCLUSION

Making Your Move Up the Ladder

Being a hard worker is an admirable trait. Unfortunately, hard work isn't always enough to propel you up the corporate ladder. If you keep your nose to the grindstone, you're likely to miss many important clues that will tell you how to find promotion opportunities in your workplace, how to create your own opportunities, and how to overcome the obstacles that could prevent you from reaching your goals.

Give yourself—and your workplace—a reality check. For example, ask yourself:

- Are you in the wrong place at the wrong time?

- Does nepotism play a role in your company?

- Would your company care if you left?

- Is there discrimination within your company (e.g., based on gender, age, race, etc.)?

- Have you correctly assessed your job performance?

Analyze your company's needs. Then think about how you do—or can—help the company meet those needs. Will a job have to be created for you if you are to be promoted? If so, develop a position paper explaining why the job should be created and why you should fill it. If the job already exists, develop a strategy to get it. Identify your strengths. If necessary, get more training or education. Make sure to bring your accomplishments to the attention of those who are in a position to promote you.

If you feel you're stuck in a job that has become intolerable, consider a lateral move within the company—but only if that move will eventually lead to your ultimate goal. Don't allow yourself to get sidetracked from your career path just to get away from a bad situation. If all else fails, start planning how to obtain a position with another organization.

ASKING FOR A RAISE OR A PROMOTION

In many organizations, your raise is part of your review. However, the amount of the raise is likely to be based on performance. In other organizations, raises are awarded on a more arbitrary basis. If your supervisor decides that you deserve a raise, you get one.

Either way, you can increase your chances of getting the raise or promotion you want. You just have to remember three basic things:

1. You must be sure you deserve it.

2. You must be sure your boss knows you deserve it.

3. You must be sure your boss knows that you know you deserve it.

Got that? Good, then you're on your way.

The first thing to do is to set up a meeting with your boss to discuss your raise or promotion. (Try not to pick the day your boss is having root canal work done.) If at all possible, schedule your meeting for early in the day or after-hours when you are less likely to be disturbed and your boss is less likely to be distracted.

Be prepared to discuss what your duties and responsibilities were when you were hired, last promoted, or last given a raise (whichever is appropriate for your situation). Although you know all the wonderful things you have accomplished, your boss may not be aware of some of them. Don't be afraid to blow your own horn. Did you save the company money? Did you increase profits or productivity? Have you been innovative in your current position? Present any documentation you can to support your list of accomplishments.

Tip: Keep a weekly list of accomplishments. By the end of the year, you may forget some of the things you've achieved unless you've written them down.

Telling the boss how hard you've worked or that you need the money is not likely to get you anywhere. You must be specific about how your work has benefited your boss and the company up until now—and how your continued success will benefit them in the future.

So, what happens if your boss turns you down? It's important to find out why you didn't get the raise or promotion. Is it your performance? If so, then what do you need to do to turn the situation around? Some bosses will offer this feedback automatically. If yours doesn't, ask for it. You may not like hearing what he or she has to say, but you need to hear it.

You may find out that it isn't you at all. The company simply may not have money to give you a raise or have a position suitable for you. If that's the case, then you should evaluate your options and decide whether you want to stay with the organization or seek a new position in an organization where there may be more opportunity for financial or professional advancement.

MANAGING REJECTION

With risk comes reward, the old adage promises. And many times that's true, particularly when it comes to your career. But what the old adage doesn't tell you is that with risk can also come rejection.

Every time you "put yourself out there," take a stand, try something new in your career, you open yourself up to the possibility of rejection. The alternative is to always "play it safe," "blend in with the crowd"—and forget about being a Promotable Person.

If the thought of rejection makes you nervous, think about these examples of people who have experienced it firsthand:

- At the age of 65, Colonel Sanders tried to sell his chicken recipe. He received more than 1,000 rejections before making millions with KFC.

- Henry Ford went bankrupt his first year in the automobile business and failed with his second company two years later. But on his third attempt, he made automotive history.

- Consider the author who called himself Dr. Seuss. His children's book was rejected by twenty-three publishers. Millions of children and their parents are thankful for publisher number twenty-four.

These are only a few of the people who have experienced rejection and gone on to achieve great success. But there are countless other stories of people who, when faced with rejection, just gave up. No one can blame them—rejection is never easy. Of course, no one remembers them either.

What sets those who succeed apart from those who don't? People who fail generally don't handle rejection well. The fact is, they often don't handle it at all. They take things personally and, instead of trying again, give up. They let fear of further rejection stop them cold before they really have a chance to be successful.

The Promotable Person learns how to take rejection in stride. One good formula to remember is this:

REFLECT—REEVALUATE—REDIRECT

Reflect. Think about what has happened. Give yourself some time to feel the pain. Your natural tendency may be to rush into an action. Don't. The action could be denial, anger, blame, or discounting your disappointment. Let yourself acknowledge any and all of these reactions in private. But think before you make a move. Time and reflection often help put things in perspective. They provide a chance to learn from the experience, analyze the situation without being blinded by emotion, and consider all options. The action that follows this period of reflection is much more likely to be positive and lead to favorable results.

Reevaluate. You have two choices. You can view the situation in a negative way and give up, be depressed, be a victim, or look for somewhere to place the blame. Or you can view the rejection as part of the learning process and ask questions, analyze the problem, get suggestions, and search for honest feedback (your mentors can be of tremendous help here).

Redirect. In other words, keep trying—but in a different way. Just because one person doesn't like something, you can't assume no one will. If necessary, try a different approach. Be creative. Learn everything you can about the needs and realities of the industry or particular organization you're trying to impress. This is a perfect opportunity to create your own opportunities. Believe it or not, the initial rejection may motivate you to take a new direction—an even better one—that you may never have thought of before.

Take the example of the young photojournalist who was employed by a major city paper. When the paper folded, she applied for numerous jobs in her field. She was rejected each time. Instead of giving up, she redirected her energies and searched for other opportunities to use her talents. Eventually, she was hired by a large pharmaceutical firm as an industrial photographer. After a year, she saw a job posted in a different field within the corporation. She applied for the job and got it. This career change has led to many promotions for this young woman, and all because she had the courage and resourcefulness to turn rejection into success.

Only you know whether you have what it takes to be a Promotable Person. If the prospect and challenge excite you, then go for it! This book provides the basic guidelines to launch you on your way. Assess your strengths. Identify the areas you need to strengthen, and then start today, right now. The sooner you begin, the sooner you will achieve your goals. You have the skills. You have the confidence. You have the power. You are the Promotable Person.

AVAILABLE FROM
SKILLPATH PUBLICATIONS

SELF-STUDY SOURCEBOOKS

Climbing the Corporate Ladder: What You Need to Know and Do to Be a Promotable Person *by Barbara Pachter and Marjorie Brody*

Mastering the Art of Communication: Your Keys to Developing a More Effective Personal Style *by Michelle Fairfield Poley*

Productivity Power: 250 Great Ideas for Being More Productive *by Jim Temme*

Promoting Yourself: 50 Ways to Increase Your Prestige, Power, and Paycheck *by Marlene Caroselli, Ed.D.*

Risk-Taking: 50 Ways to Turn Risks Into Rewards *by Marlene Caroselli, Ed.D. and David Harris*

Total Quality Customer Service: How to Make It Your Way of Life *by Jim Temme*

Write It Right! A Guide for Clear and Correct Writing *by Richard Andersen and Helene Hinis*

SPIRAL HANDBOOKS

The ABC's of Empowered Teams: Building Blocks for Success *by Mark Towers*

Breaking the Ice: How to Improve Your On-the-Spot Communication Skills *by Deborah Shouse*

Dynamic Delegation! A Manager's Guide for Active Empowerment *by Mark Towers*

Every Woman's Guide to Career Success *by Denise M. Dudley*

Hiring and Firing: What Every Manager Needs to Know *by Marlene Caroselli, Ed.D. with Laura Wyeth, Ms.Ed.*

How to Deal With Difficult People *by Paul Friedman*

Learning to Laugh at Work: The Power of Humor in the Workplace
by Robert McGraw

Making Your Mark: How to Develop a Personal Marketing Plan for Becoming
More Visible and More Appreciated at Work *by Deborah Shouse*

Meetings That Work *by Marlene Caroselli, Ed.D.*

The Mentoring Advantage: How to Help Your Career Soar to New Heights
by Pam Grout

NameTags Plus: Games You Can Play When People Don't Know What to Say
by Deborah Shouse

Networking: How to Creatively Tap Your People Resources *by Colleen Clarke*

New & Improved! 25 Ways to Be More Creative and More Effective
by Pam Grout

Power Write! A Practical Guide to Words That Work *by Helene Hinis*

Putting Anger to Work For You! *by Ruth and Joel Schroeder*

Reinventing Your Self: 28 Strategies for Coping With Change *by Mark Towers*

The Supervisor's Guide: The Everyday Guide to Coordinating People and Tasks
by Jerry Brown and Denise Dudley, Ph.D.

Taking Charge: A Personal Guide to Managing Projects and Priorities
by Michal E. Feder

Treasure Hunt: 10 Stepping Stones to a New and More Confident You!
by Pam Grout

A Winning Attitude: How to Develop Your Most Important Asset!
by Michelle Fairfield Poley

For more information, call 1-800-873-7545.